BEAST OF THE EAST

Penn State vs Pitt

A game-by-game history of America's greatest football rivalry

By Tim Panaccio

Leisure Press
P.O. Box 3
West Point, NY 10996

Library of Congress Catalog Card Number 82-81808
ISBN 0-88011-068-6
Printed in the United States

All photos in this book unless otherwise specified have been
reproduced through the efforts of both school's archives
department, the University of Pittsburgh and Pennsylvania State
University. Most of these photos have never appeared in book form
until now.

Table of Contents

Foreword

His hair was more white than gray.

He was old; you could tell by the way he negotiated the stairs. He limped badly; a woman, younger in years than he, held his left arm. Together, they descended the long, long steel flight of steps outside Beaver Stadium's press box.

We had taken the stairs that afternoon instead of the elevator. Too crowded, too long a wait. "What the hell, let's walk," I suggested to Rick.

He was moving very slowly when we finally caught up to him.

"Rip," she said softly, "let's move over so the boys can pass."

He moved to the right, she smiled, we thanked her.

I looked back as we passed him, though not in quite so much a hurry now to get down those stairs. He sort of winked at me. I could see the pain in his eyes. The stairs would be his greatest adversary that afternoon.

"Do you know who that was?" Rick asked me as we neared the bottom of our descent.

"I think so," I replied. "Rip Engle, wasn't it?"

"Yeah. Boy, did he look bad."

Some years later, when I was a sportswriter for the *Philadelphia Journal,* I had dinner with Rick Starr at the Park Schenley in Pittsburgh. Rick was the sports editor of the Valley News Dispatch. We reminisced about our days as student-reporters for the Penn State *Daily Collegian.* Though neither of us ever cared to admit it, we were haunted by what had happened that gray afternoon in Beaver Stadium. We both knew we had blown a better story on that staircase than the one we got in the Penn State dressing room that day.

You could always listen to Joe. Joe always had something to say. We filled volumes with Joe Paterno quotes before we graduated. Why, we wondered, did we pass Rip that day without ever caring to stop and talk? I still don't know.

As I wrote this book, which is not so much about Penn State football as it is about the historic rivalry between Penn State and Pitt, I thought about that meeting on the staircase.

And because two newspapers, the *Journal* and *Philadelphia Bulletin,* had folded during the time I was writing, I thought about the many familiar faces who had covered so many of these games. Faces I'd never see again. Like the *Bulletin's* Frank Bilovsky, whom I had run quotes for during Penn State games in the early '70s when I was still a student there.

More than any other Eastern football rivalry, Pitt-Penn State has, over the years, taken on a meaning entirely its own. Like the major collegiate rivalries of its day, this one leaves an everlasting impression upon you because in Pennsylvania, this is the *only* game that really counts, year-in, year-out. Records don't mean a thing. Just who wins this game.

In researching 81 years of Pitt-Penn State games, I ran across some fascinating characters who played at these two schools. This book has attempted to expand upon some of them and merge them into the total picture that is Pitt vs. Penn State. I didn't write 81 games stories. I've linked them, I hope, to the past and, in some cases, the future. What I ended up with is an 81-game novel.

The back of the book contains a page listing my many sources of information, for which I am grateful. Special thanks go to Penn State Sports Information Director Dave Baker, and Pitt's Joyce Ashenbrenner and Kimball Smith. Like anything else, in order to have an end, you need a beginning. For me, they were the beginning.

The Free Library of Philadelphia and Carnegie Library in Pittsburgh provided the complete 81 years of newspaper microfilm which were needed. Naturally, every author has an editor to proof the final manuscript. Mine was the *Philadelphia Daily News'* Rich Hofmann.

Biggest thanks of all go to my wife, Carla, and parents for enabling me to write this book without ever having to baby-sit my son, Nicolas, or worry about his wandering whereabouts around the house.

Tim Panaccio

To
Carla, who persevered during
months when this was written.

1893

Game 1

Aim for the Trees

On Nov. 6, 1893 the world, for the most part, was a peaceful place. The Sino-Japanese War in which Japan would become an imperial power was still a year away.

In Chicago, it was a time for celebration as the Windy City was hosting the World's Columbian Exposition.

For Americans, it was a time to forget about their troubles. The scarcity of gold had thrown the nation into a financial panic. Thousands of banks and commercial businesses would close before the economic recovery in 1897.

Grover Cleveland had been in office nearly a year and the hard times that were just beginning fell on his shoulders. Rumors surfaced that the Populists would replace the Democrats as the second major party in the United States.

In the quiet town of State College, Pa., which was then a borough of Bellefonte, two collegiate football teams lined up against each other for the first time. Eighty more such meetings would take place, though few foresaw such on this snowy afternoon.

The men in Blue & White represented State College. Their foes hailed from Pittsburgh. Western University of Pennsylvania, they called themselves, WUP for short. From this game, the richest, most colorful and bitter college football rivalry in Pennsylvania would plant its seeds among Americana—Pitt vs. Penn State.

The *Pittsburg(h) Press* heralded the event the following day with

11

The Western University Eleven Failed to Score.

TREES IN THE PLAY,

But the Bellefonte Boys Showed Up in Much Stronger Form Than the Ambitious Visitors From Pittsburg—The Official Result Was 32 to 0.

BELLEFONTE, Nov. 7.—

YESTERDAY the Western University of Pennsylvania was defeated by the Pennsylvania state college strong eleven on the home grounds in a football game of 30-minute halves by the score of 32 to 0. State college took the ball but fumbled, and the Western team pushed them back to their 25-guard line, and for nearly 15 minutes the ball was in state college territory. It was soon, by strong dashes and long runs by White, taken over the Western line for a touchdown, and shortly it was again rushed over for a second touchdown, after which the half ended, score 12 to 0. In the second half the ball was nearly all the time in the Western's territory, though considerable punting was indulged in on both sides. Touchdowns were made by rushers twice, and once Neal fumbled, Dunsmore falling on the ball, scoring a touchdown in the last few minutes. Neal made a safety, saving another down. Good work was done by White, Dowler and Stuart for state college, and by McNeil, Fiscus, Trees and Boden for Western. The summary is as follows:

W. U. P.—0.	Positions.	P. A. C.—32.
Price	Left end	Harris
Marchand	Left tackle	J. Dunsmore
Hill	Left guard	Fisher
Hull	Center	George
Fiscus	Right guard	Dowler
Trees	Right tackle	W. Dunsmore
Marshall	Right end	White
Rose	Quarter back	McCasky
McNeil	Right half-back	Haley
Neal	Left half-back	Atherton
Flower (Boden)	Full back	Stuart

Touchdowns: Stuart 1, Atherton 1, Dunsmore 1, Haley 2. Goals: Atherton 5. Safety: Neal. Referee: McLean. Umpire: Gill.

W. U. P. COMMENT.

The 'Varsity Boys Were Royally Entertained Yesterday.

this headline: "The Western University Eleven Failed to Score." Tucked underneath was a clever ditty: "Trees In The Play."

Someone from State College might have interpreted that subhead to mean the playing field was cluttered with dutch elms or pines. But to the Pittsburgh sports fan, "Trees" meant Pitt's right tackle. Trees' first name was omitted and doesn't appear on the Panther roll call even today.

This game also marked the dedication of the grandstand at Beaver Field which seated 500, had an overhanging roof and three flagpoles. Originally scheduled for November 4, the game was postponed two days to Monday because of heavy snow.

The Penn State student publication, *Free Lance*, reported: "When the boys from Allegheny arrived, they found the vilest kind of weather and agreed to the postponement." University officials housed Pitt's players with several fraternities over the long weekend.

Naturally, a good bit of old fashioned Penn State partying took place. In fact, it is said that Penn State's reputation as a "party school" in part can be traced to this infamous weekend when Pitt's football team unwound.

All that fun seemed to have left Pitt exhausted. Penn State battered the Panthers, 32-0. And who says university officials didn't know what they were doing when it came time to house Pitt?

The Nittany Lions fumbled in the opening minutes and were pushed back to their own 25-yard line before Beaver White (no connection to the field which was named after General James Adams Beaver, former University president) ripped off several long gains as Penn State took a 6-0 lead that would become 12-0 at the half.

Right halfback Ed Haley finished the game with two touchdowns and left halfback Charles Atherton, fullback W. A. Stuart and right tackle William Dunsmore all tallied for Penn State. WUP's left halfback, Neal, was tackled for a safety. That's all we know about the first Pitt-Penn State clash, now an annual tradition in Pennsylvania.

Neither school's coach was quoted in the *Press*, which is unfortunate because this game marked the first and last meeting between State Coach George Hoskins and WUP's Anson Harrold. Harrold was fired after a 1-4 rookie season. Hoskins' record was the reverse.

Oddly enough, the *Press* sought out umpire Gill to enlighten the readers of the day on the game.

"For the University," Gill began, "Trees broke up the interference and tackled to perfection. The gains of McNeil helped to advance the ball far into State College's territory. DuBarry's tackling was fine.

Pitt's team, circa 1890s. Shown in the background are Pitt's football barracks.

Penn State team, 1893.

George Hoskin, Penn State's first Head Coach and, later, Pitt Head Coach.

Hill played like a demon and got through the line to stop many a buck.

"The strong point of the State College team is its powerful line, against which the University could not stand ... Capt. Haley, the 190-pound halfback of State College, smashed up against the University line like a thunderbolt and never failed to make the required gain."

Gill politely noted that Haley's yardage was directed at Trees. True, Mr. Trees was involved in many plays, but that's because Penn State had run right over him.

1896

Game 2

Brotherly Tradition

When the series resumed in 1896, Dr. Samuel Newton had taken over the coaching reins at Penn State while George Hoskins, the man who led State to its first-ever victory over Pitt, had switched schools after compiling a 17-4-4 four-year record.

Penn State again was victorious at Beaver Field, this time 10-4. Sounds like a baseball score but keep in mind that during the primitive (or is it formative?) years of football, only four points were awarded for a touchdown and two for the point after. Field goals and safeties counted two points.

The average reader practically needed a magnifying glass to find the results of this game in the Sunday *Pittsburgh Press*, Oct. 4, 1896. The story was buried among the *Press'* football roundup, which was broken up by several crude drawings depicting the action of the day, so to speak.

Right halfback, J. A. Dunsmore, the second of three brothers who lettered at Penn State, carried the Lion attack and scored both touchdowns. A fellow named Ensminger kicked one point while Clarence Thompson missed the other.

Although Mr. Marshall of Pitt scored the lone Panther touchdown, the highlight of the afternoon was Dunsmore's rushing efforts.

Dunsmore's first carry resulted in a 40-yard gain and he eventually moved the Lions to the Pitt five-yard line before Penn State turned the ball over on a fumble.

J. A. Dunsmore, Penn State halfback, 1896.

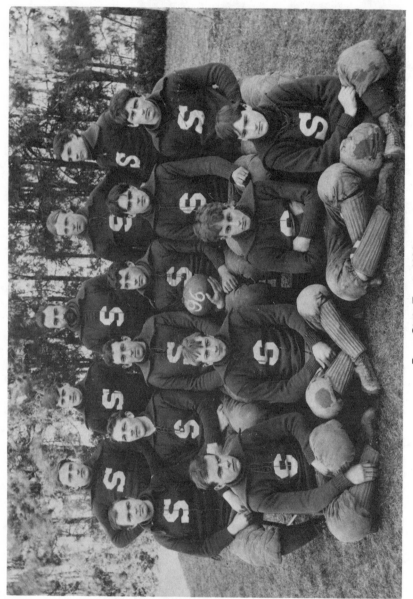

Penn State Team, 1896.

The *Press* reporter covering the game wrote that most of the first half was played at midfield. "A hard tussle," he termed it. Near the end of the half, however, Dunsmore broke loose for Penn State's first score.

Dunsmore carried the Lions in the second half on a 50-yard drive that culminated in his second touchdown and Ensminger's successful PAT, making it 10-4. Sandwiched in there was Marshall's score for Pitt.

Although there was no mention of inclement weather, for some reason the second half was cut from 20 to 15 minutes.

Of historical note is the fact that Panther Coach George Hoskins played the entire way at center.

Neither Penn State nor Pitt had an outstanding season, finishing 3-4 and 3-6 respectively. Four years later when these two titans again met, Pop Golden was coaching the Lions and Dr. Roy Jackson the Panthers.

1900

Game 3

WUPs Whupped

Roy Jackson was just delighted after Pitt lost 12-0 to Penn State at Beaver Field.

How do we know that Dr. Jackson was delighted? Because the *Pittsburgh Press* headline said so.

Actually, the headline had taken Jackson's post-game comments out of context. What he told reporters was that he was pleased with the way Pitt had played in its season opener.

Pitt's administrators weren't delighted, however, with Jackson's coaching. He was gone after a 5-4 season.

A heavy downpour in Bellefonte limited the game to 35 minutes, but that was plenty of time for fullback Ralph Cummings and left guard Henry Scholl to score for Penn State.

After an exchange of punts, Penn State drove on Pitt for nearly 15 minutes with "a succession of line plunges of the fiercest kind," according to the *Press* sportswriter.

Cummings bolted over for the Lions' first score and Percival Martin added the PAT to give State a 6-0 lead. Cummings finished the half with a nifty 20-yard run, but Penn State failed to widen its lead.

The remainder of the story gets a bit tricky. One thing is fairly certain: both teams had trouble holding onto the ball in the rain. Pitt's second fumble of the second half gave Penn State the ball on the Panther 10-yard line, where Scholl eventually succeeded in crossing the goal line. Martin's kick accounted for the 12-0 final score.

It is not known how much of a weight advantage Penn State enjoyed in this game, but it was apparently significant enough to cause the *Press'* headline writer to mention it as a sub-head over the story: "WUP Kickers Were Much Lighter Than Their Opponents, But Did Well."

FOOTBALL AT STATE COLLEGE

TWO TOUCH-DOWNS WERE MADE AGAINST THE WESTERN UNIVERSITY ELEVEN.

THE FINAL SCORE OF THE GAME WAS 12 TO 0.

W. U. P. KICKERS WERE MUCH LIGHTER THAN THEIR OPPONENTS, BUT DID WELL.

COACH JACKSON DELIGHTED.

Ralph Cummings, Penn State fullback, 1900.

1901

Game 4

What's the Final Score?

William McKinley, the 25th President of the United States, had been dead 15 days when Pitt traveled to Bellefonte on Sept. 29 to meet Penn State. The news of McKinley's assassination, the third American leader to be gunned down at the time, would fill newspapers for the remainder of the month.

Both the *Philadelphia Inquirer* and *Pittsburgh Press* continued to roll banner headlines across the front pages of their respective newspapers, updating the McKinley funeral proceedings with reaction from around the nation and the world. Among the major metropolitan papers at the time, only the *Press* covered the 1901 Pitt-Penn State clash.

One curious item about this game concerns the final score. The *Press* reported Penn State as having won 37-0. No one challenged that State won this game. Problem was, no one could agree on the score.

Football records at Pitt show the score as being both 33-0 and 27-0; the latter score also appears in Penn State's football press guides. In compiling this book, the author studied the thinly-sketched details of the game and using the accompanying box-score, has concluded that the final score *should* have been 36-0.

William N. (Pop) Golden, Penn State Head Coach, 1900 to 1902.

Pop Golden (left) and his successor, Dan Reed. Reed coached one year and eventually became a New York Congressman.

One thing is certain—Pitt was embarrassed by Pop Golden's Lions. "Though the visitors played a plucky game all through," the *Press* reported, "they were entirely outclassed by State's heavier team, superior work and good physical condition of the men. At no time did the visitors come near scoring."

Penn State ran right around Pitt's defensive ends as Henry Scholl piled up the yardage and provided the Lions' first touchdown just three minutes into the game. Although a tackle, Scholl would score three times against Pitt.

Scholl's second touchdown that half gave Penn State an 8-0 lead. Left halfback Ed Whitworth's 45- and 15-yard bursts set up the TD.

According to the *Press'* account, Penn State continued to blitz Pitt along the line in the second half while racking up six more touchdowns. Whitworth is credited with having scored three times, with one each to quarterback Earl Hewitt, Sr., right halfback Robert Bennett, and Scholl.

Given kicker Sam Russell's two successful PATs, Penn State apparently scored 28 second-half points, which would have made the final score 36-0.

But who's going to argue? Coach Wilbur Hockensmith made sure his Panthers recovered from this opening game loss as Pitt's final 7-2-1 log would indicate. Penn State, on the other hand, finished 5-4.

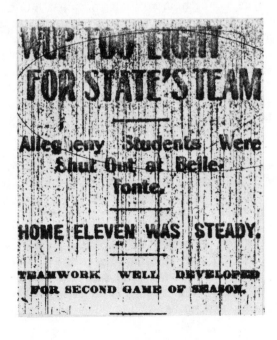

1902

Game 5

Not Worth the Space

Perhaps the most fascinating aspect of the Pitt-Penn State series is the amount of coverage, or lack thereof, newspapers devoted to the game, particularly during the early 1900s when the rivalry, if you dare call it that, was being nurtured through its infancy.

The *Philadelphia Bulletin* and *Inquirer* devoted little or no coverage to this game for nearly 27 years. Ditto in Pittsburgh, where the morning *Post-Gazette*, *Sun-Telegraph* and evening *Press* paid only cursory attention to what would someday become the biggest annual football game in the East, with the possible exception of Army-Navy.

You'd have to search long and hard to find the single paragraph the *Press* devoted to the 1902 "classic," won by Penn State, 27-0. Even lowly high school games received more space—quadruple the amount, in fact—than this game.

Still, the one paragraph the *Press* ran on the game was one more than any newspaper in Philadelphia devoted on Sept. 28, 1902.

The following is a verbatim account of the game as taken from the *Press*:

State College, Bellefonte, Pa., Sept. 27—By the score of 27-0, State won her second game here today by defeating the W.U. of P. The W.U.P.'s were weakened by the absence of three of their best men. Their team was pounds lighter than State and they were at a further disadvantage owing to the muddy field. They put up a good, stubborn game, several times making long gains around State's ends and breaking through the line for the distance. For the visitors, Boyd, Douglass and Martin were the stars, while Smith, Dean, Hewitt and McIlveen played best for State.

According to the boxscore, left halfback Irish McIlveen scored two touchdowns to pace the Lion attack. McIlveen's back-up, Carl Forkum, added another score, as did tackle Brit Seeley and fullback Andy Smith.

One interesting item—this was the last game played in State College until 1931. The next 28 would be played in Pittsburgh.

1903

Game 6

Tex Gets Stung

This was to be Arthur "Texas" Mosse's grand introduction to big-time football. Mosse had just assumed command at Pitt. The poor chap had no idea that an 0-8-1 season loomed on the horizon.

Nor did Mosse ever envision losing to Penn State 59-0 in mid-season at Exposition Park. Things were so bad for Pitt, that despite Penn State's objections, Mosse inserted himself into the Panther line-up in the first half. It was duly noted that were it not for Mosse's presence on the field, Pitt would have surrendered considerably more points.

One writer described Pitt's annihilation in these words: ". . . the W.U.P's were like babes in the embrace of giants."

The giant, as it was, came in the form of Penn State's Carl Forkum. The junior fullback had a marvelous game scoring five touchdowns and connecting on nine of 10 PATs. Forkum's 38 points is the most scored by any player in the Pitt-Penn State series. It's also a Nittany Lion school record.

Pitt was doomed from the start as Mosse's first-half fumble gave Penn State the ball on the Panther 30-yard line. Tackle James Arbuthnot and Forkum ran the ball to the 16 before Forkum finally struck paydirt, then booted his own extra point for a 6-0 lead.

Pitt's second drive of the game stalled out near mid-field. On the takeover, the duo of Forkum and senior halfback Ed Whitworth worked it inside the Panther 30 before Irv Thompson scored the first

Irish McIlveen, Penn State halfback. Scored twice in the 1903 game.

Carl Forkum, Penn State fullback, 1903.

of his three touchdowns on the day, this one from 26 yards away. Just for good measure, Thompson kicked his own PAT for a 12-0 Lion advantage.

The game continued this trend for over three hours. Penn State would score, Pitt would move a couple of yards, then punt and the Lions would roar right back into the end zone. Forkum closed out the half with a brilliant 56-yard scamper to the Panther 9, then followed with a touchdown on the next snap from center. Following his point-after, it was 18-0.

Penn State got the ball back minutes later. This time it was Irish McIlveen's turn to do a jig on the Panthers' front line, which was left wheezing every time a Lion gushed past them.

McIlveen blazed 52 yards for yet another touchdown and a 24-0 halftime lead.

Lion Coach Dan Reed, who was celebrating his first season at the helm, substituted liberally in the second half but failed to stifle his boys' impulse for running up the score.

Forkum, Thompson and McIlveen paced a 52-yard drive to open the second half, running right through Pitt's tackles, and staked Penn State to a 30-0 lead on Forkum's third score.

Penn State's magic formula—running the ball through the tackles—continued to work wonders as Mosse searched vainly for a solution. He tried to lift his team's spirits by tackling with reckless abandon, but all that energy spent was futile. The Lions simply couldn't be stopped.

Thompson's 39-yard score made it 36-0. Forkum then responded with a 30-yard score of his own on the following series. McIlveen went 41 yards minutes later, then allowed Forkum, who was visibly tired at this point, to dive over from just feet away for his fifth—and thankfully, last—score, giving State a 46-0 pad. Thompson racked up two more touchdowns in the waning minutes, accounting for the Lions' 59 points.

Penn State ended the season with a 5-3 record and in case you're wondering if the 59 margin was a record for worst defeats, well it was for a while.

But the all-time granddaddy of roll 'em up scores in Nittany Lion history would occur September 24, 1921 when Penn State humiliated Lebanon Valley, 109-7.

In retrospect, Tex Mosse got off easy.

1904

GAME 7

Give It to Judd and O.H.

When Teddy Roosevelt delivered his State of the Union address in 1904, he reiterated America's previous commitment to maintain law and order in Latin America.

It's not known how Pitt Coach Texas Mosse addressed his players prior to this game, but it's safe to say he demanded some restoration of peace, law and order following Penn State's 59-0 massacre in 1903.

Penn State entered the game a virtual cripple, without running back Carl Forkum, the Lions' acknowledged offensive catalyst, as well as massive tackle Andy Moscript and tight end Charles Campbell. Before the day ended, Pitt would claim its first series victory 22-5, and the Lions would lose two more players to injury, halfback Ed Yeckley and end Cal Moorehead, who played most of the game with a splintered collarbone.

Pitt's double-dynamite backfield of Judd Schmidt and O.H. Mehl scored two touchdowns which, incidentally, now counted for five points, while State's only tally came from fullback George McGee.

The Panthers scored three first-half touchdowns to take a commanding 17-0 lead and then coasted the remainder of the way behind the running of Schmidt, who delighted 8,500 visitors to Exposition Park, particularly with a 67-yard run on a muddy field.

The win marked Pitt's first undefeated season (10-0).

Penn State, under first-year Coach Tom Fennell, started the game with a decent drive, aided mostly by McIlveen's 35-yard kickoff return to midfield. But the Panther line held thereafter, forcing the Lions to punt.

Joe Thompson fielded McIlveen's punt at the Panther 15 and ran it back 40 yards. Thompson, Mehl and Schmidt then battered their way downfield into Lion territory. From the Penn State 35-yard line, Mehl took the ball on a double lateral and ran 30 yards to the Lion 5. On third down, Schmidt cracked over from the one, giving Pitt a 5-0 lead. Joe Edgar's point-after made it 6-0.

Schmidt and Mehl added two more TD's, accounting for Pitt's 17-0 intermission score.

Thomson ignited Pitt's second-half attack with two spectacular runs, the first a 30-yard kickoff return, followed quickly by a 21-yard burst around the end, placing the ball inside the Penn State 40-yard line. Schmidt took it from there on first down all the way to the 4 before Mehl's rush into the line made it 22-0.

WON THE GAME BY TEAM WORK

W. U. P. Outplayed State Eleven In Every Department

SOME SPECTACULAR RUNS.

SUBSTITUTES ALLOWED VISITORS TO SCORE IN SECOND HALF.

FINAL SCORE WAS 22 TO 5.

At this point, Mosse, who seemed to have recovered from the previous year's humiliation, substituted freely. Reporters of the day noted that were it not for the scrubs entering the game, it's doubtful whether Penn State would have crossed the Panthers' goal line.

The Lions' only score arrived shortly after Mosse's wholesale subs were in the game. Driving from the Panther 40 after Pitt failed to make the required first-down yardage, McIlveen took Penn State inside the 10 before yielding to Forkum's replacement in this game, George McGee, who scored Penn State's five points.

Pitt nearly added another late TD when Penn State fumbled it away inside its own 12-yard line, but time expired.

Although the sportwriter who covered the game for the *Pittsburgh Press* remained anonymous, his last paragraph reeked of biased reporting:

> . . . The State team was so inferior to W.U.P. yesterday, so that it is hard to pick out any individuals that starred for the Blue and Gold, but much credit must be given East and Perry, the ends.

Funny thing is, in the fifth paragraph of the story, the *Press* reporter tells his readers who the true unsung heroes of the contest were:

> . . . Moorehead displayed great grit and he, with McIlveen, were the best performers on the State team.

A word about Joe Thompson: Upon his graduation in 1905, he joined the Panther coaching staff and later coached the 1910 team to an undefeated, untied (9-0), unscored-upon season. Thompson would also become a World War I hero.

1905

Game 8

A Small Piece of Glory

Among the many individual heroes in the long history of the Pitt-Penn State series, there is one whose name went largely unnoticed—Irish McIlveen. You won't find him in the Nittany Lion record books, except on the Penn State lettermen roll call.

Consider for a moment that Carl Forkum once scored five touchdowns and kicked nine extra points against Pitt in 1903 and failed to make the books until recently when his achievement was unearthed.

Charles Atherton scored only one touchdown in the series, yet the University named a bulding after him and the Borough of State College graced him with a street title.

Irish McIlveen was not so lucky, and all he did in four meetings against Pitt was score five touchdowns, and account for two of the longest runs (52 and 41 yards) from scrimmage.

The one-column, two-deck headline on the afternoon of Dec. 1, 1905 in the *Pittsburgh Press* said flatly, "STATE WINS GREAT GAME." It was a titanic struggle between two teams that refused to yield ground.

Penn State won, 6-0, when McIlveen barrelled into the end zone with just six seconds remaining in the first half.

McIlveen also punted six times for 193 yards. That's an average of 32 yards, which wasn't very spectacular, especially when you consider Pitt's Judd Schmidt compiled 225 yards on the same number

Charles Atherton, Penn State player. Atherton Hall at State College is named after him.

STATE WINS
GREAT GAME

Center County Lads Held by Locals to a Single Touchdown

of attempts. But the point here is that McIlveen was your basic all-around player who so typified football's most chaotic period, when rules were changing every season, players went both ways at various positions, and seldom left the lineup unless severely injured.

Time and again McIlveen, fullback George Yeckley and halfback George McGee dented the Pitt line but when push came to shove, the Panthers refused to cave-in. Several drives by both teams stalled out within scoring distance.

From the game account, we can safely say Penn State mounted the better attack.

"W.U.P. put up a plucky fight, but nothing could resist the awful onslaughts of State's backs," reported the *Press*. ". . . W.U.P. held hard at critical stages, and State had to fight like demons for their touchdown."

It was a defensive battle to the end and most Pittsburghers who viewed the action at Exposition Park were not surprised at the outcome because Penn State had the bigger squad. The Lions finished the season 8-3 while the Panthers were 10-2, scored 406 points and limited their opponents to a mere 36.

Panther Coach Texas Mosse was never dubbed "a defensive specialist," but in two of his three years at the school, he turned a club that had given up 262 points in his rookie year, into a defensive behemoth that surrendered just 41 over the course of his last two seasons.

As irony would have it, it was Penn State which had ruined Pitt's scoreless game string (nine games) in 1904 when the Lions scored five points on McGee's late touchdown with McIlveen blocking. Recall that Mosse pulled his first unit in the second half of that game and then State scored. No one would have faulted Mosse had he kept his starters in the lineup, thus assuring Pitt of having held its opponents scoreless. But Texas Mosse wasn't that kind of coach. Records didn't mean all that much to him. The only other team besides State to score on the Panthers in 1905 was Cornell, which romped to a 30-0 victory.

Pitt's team photo, 1905.

Texas Mosse steped down after 1905 and E. R. Wingard took over, though for only one season. Historically speaking, 1905 was equally important to remember because there had been 14 fatalities in football that year and 71 total since that turn of the century.

Outraged by a newspaper photograph showing a battered player, President Teddy Roosevelt demanded the game be made safer. On Dec. 28, 1905, representatives from 62 colleges convened and instituted sweeping changes in the game. The man who authored many of them was Georgia Tech Coach John Wilhelm Heisman.

Charles Atherton had a university building and street named after him. John Wilhelm Heisman's name appears on college football's most coveted trophy.

Irish McIlveen was forced to settle for a small piece of glory reserved in the annals of Pitt-Penn State football history.

1906

Game 9

The Big Brute Lost It for Us

They were called the Banbury Brothers. Quincy and William. Little Ban and Big Ban. They played for the Panthers from 1905 to 1908, although neither lettered in 1906.

Their contribution to the Pitt-Penn State series is in itself singular, not plural. Pitt lost at Exposition Park in this game 6-0 largely because of an unsportsmanlike conduct penalty on William. It's a shame that the name Banbury should be held in infamous standing because, by most accounts, Big Ban was a gentle sort who seemed quite incapable of the terrible deed he supposedly commited on Nov. 29, 1906. Namely, that of slugging a Penn State player.

We'll allow the *Pittsburgh Press* reporter to describe the scene:

In the second half W.U.P. had the advantage until within a few minutes of the close, when a most unfortunate happening helped State to a touchdown. The ball was in State's possession on W.U.P.'s 20-yard line. State made a few yards and it was here that W. Banbury was accused by Head Linesman Ed Young of slugging, and removed from the game, W.U.P. being penalized half the distance to the goal . . .

Halfback Bill McCleary scored on third down, his own PAT making it 6-0. The clock expired only seconds later. Needless to say, it was an emotionally draining game for both teams. For such a

W. T. "Mother" Dunn, Penn State's first All-American, 1906.

GREAT GAME

The Only Score Was Made With Two Minutes to Play—Wup's Strength Surprising

PENALTY HELPED STATE WIN

contest to end in controversy, however, made it all the more disturbing to the Pitt players, who complained loudly to the linesman that Banbury was one of the cleanest chaps on the gridiron and would never punch out another player. So incensed was Pitt, that a real donnybrook nearly erupted in the course of the argument between the officials and players.

The victory sealed Penn State's 8-1-1 season. Again, the *Press* felt compelled to cushion the loss with headlines that left no doubt Penn State was a heavy favorite. For instance, ". . . W.U.P.'s Strength Surprising."

Even their reporter made casual mention throughout his article that Pitt had taken on a vastly superior team, one which had given up its only points during a 10-0 loss to Yale.

"Those who had predicted that State would have no trouble in winning by a score of from 12 to 24 to 0 were certainly given a rude jolt," the *Press* stated. ". . . W.U.P. fought so desperately and tried so hard that shouts and cheers for Captain Marshall's men were heard from even the State stands."

Amid all this tumult and shouting, Penn State emerged the victor while taking an 8-1 series lead.

Lion center W. T. (Mother) Dunn was selected as the school's first All-American. Dunn would later become a prominent physician in Hawaii.

1907

Game 10

Quincy, You're All Right

Quincy Banbury's brother, William, had been a goat the year before when an unsportsmanlike conduct penalty gave Penn State the ball inside the Pitt 10-yard line, setting up Bill McCleary's game-winning touchdown.

The mighty Quince had all winter to think about his brother's misdeed. As irony would have it, Quincy Banbury was involved in the *winning* six points on Nov. 29, 1907 at Exposition Park.

"Little Ban," as his mates called him, was a hero of sorts in this, the second year of something called the "forward pass."

The final seconds of play were approaching and it appeared Penn State would return home having secured a 0-0 tie from Pitt. Panther Coach John Moorhead pulled his starting fullback, O. H. Mehl, inserting J. F. Campbell in his place with Pitt trying one, last time from the Lion 40-yard line.

A fellow by the name of Swenson was quarterbacking the Panthers in this game. Pitt's final play called for a pass to Banbury. Swenson took the snap from center, drifted back past the 40 and threw to Banbury, who caught the ball at the 10, then watched helplessly as it slipped from his grasp. The ball wobbled into the end zone. A live fumble.

The 11,000 in attendance were cheering madly as players scrambled for the loose ball. When the officials dug through the pileup, they found Campbell on top of the football. Time had expired, but

Quincy Banbury, Pitt halfback, 1907.

John Morehead, Pitt Head Coach, 1907.

FRANK VAN DOREN, D.O., Pittsburg.

American School of Osteopathy, 1903.
Varsity Football, '07, '08, '09.
Phi Rho Sigma.
Track Team, '07, '08.

"The noblest Roman of them all." Our big brother responds to a number of aliases—"Doc," "Van," "Mabel," "Grandpa," etc. As an athlete he has brought many honors to our University, his work on the gridiron last fall being especially commendable.

Frank Van Doren, Pitt, 1907 to 1909.

Pitt had scored the only points needed for victory.

Thousands swarmed onto the field to carry their heroes off. And although Quincy Banbury had nearly added more infamous legend to the family name, he was all smiles.

That night, at Pitt's football dinner, Quincy's teammates gave him a vote of confidence by electing "Little Ban" team captain for the coming season.

1908

Game 11

Stress the Defense

America had a new leader in William Howard Taft, and Pitt had a new head football coach in Joe Thompson.

Over 9,000 people ignored an early Thanksgiving afternoon shower to watch Penn State defeat Pitt, 12-6 at Exposition Park, as Larry Vorhis kicked four field goals through the uprights, only one of which was via placement.

A series of fumbles and missed opportunities doomed the Panthers. Even though the Pitt defense gave way to Penn State's running attack, it refused to yield a touchdown. Still, nothing could be done about Vorhis' toe.

Perhaps the single most exciting play of the game was Frank Van Doren's 38-yard return off a Penn State interception. Van Doren, according to game accounts, was a one-man wrecking crew, playing the role of two-way tackle.

A fierce wind blew the ball off the tee twice at the start. Penn State's first drive died just across the 50-yard line but Vorhis surprised Pitt with a fake punt, running around end for 14 yards and a Lion first down at the Panther 30. Quarterback Burke Hermann's first attempted pass of the game was fumbled away and Pitt recovered.

The ball exchanged hands twice more before State took advantage of John Lindsay's shanked punt which traveled 15 yards with Pitt backed up to the goal line. Vorhis promptly stepped onto the

Larry Vorhis, Penn State field goal specialist, 1908.

field and booted a field goal.

His second field goal of the first half gave the Lions a 6-0 lead before Van Doren drove the Panthers 72 yards with J. F. Campbell going over for the touchdown.

Both teams ran the ball on each other in the second half but neither found a way into the end zone. That, of course, was of little consequence to Vorhis, who twice booted field goals from 20 yards out to ensure Penn State's 12-6 victory.

Vorhis had one of his many punts blocked by Van Doren when the latter crashed into him, secured the football and then rambled upfield, dragging Vorhis alongside.

Pitt's touchdown did not come easy. Two completions by Panther quarterback Norman Budd toward the end of the 72-yard drive placed the ball at the Lion 2-yard line. State remained unconvinced, however, that Budd's second pass had garnered the necessary first-down yardage and requested a measurement.

The tape revealed Pitt had just enough distance. The following play, Campbell ran through George Bailey's block into the end zone.

A trend seemed to be developing in these games. Points were hard to come by. Since 1905, only 36 points had been scored in four games. Between 1904 and 1911 a mere 52 points would be registered in six games between these two clubs, an average of less than nine a game.

What a striking contrast this offered when you consider that 149 points were scored in four successive games prior to 1905. Defensive football, it appeared, had overtaken the Pitt-Penn State series.

1909

Game 12

A Tribute to State

Bill Hollenback, Penn State's new head coach, had to feel somewhat remorseful prior to the 1909 encounter with Pitt. The Lions were one victory away from a 5-0-2 season. More significantly, they would lose to graduation the services of three outstanding players—Burke Hermann, Bill "Bull" McCleary, and Larry Vorhis.

For one of the few times in its early history, this November meeting produced good weather. "Ideal conditions" said the *Pittsburgh Press*. When it was over, Penn State had escaped Forbes Field with a 5-0 win. Bull McCleary furnished the points with his first-half touchdown.

Penn State should have scored more points, considering it racked up 181 yards rushing compared to Pitt's meager 22. Pitt failed to get a first down too, while Penn State had 11. Things didn't improve in the final 35 minutes although Pitt outgained Penn State 60-54 and won the battle of first downs, 2-1.

There's a funny line in the *Press* story referring to Panther quarterback Bill Robinson. ". . . Robinson wore the stars for the locals," the story said, "the sturdy little quarterback playing as if his life depended upon it."

Robinson supplied even more entertainment with his electrifying runbacks off punts, which the story said, "kept the crowd on its feet, yelling like mad half the time."

Vorhis, the usually-reliable Lion kicker, blew a chip shot field goal

49

Bull McCleary, Penn State, 1909.

FOOT BALL

CAPT. McCLEARY

Penn State starting backfield, 1909: Bull McCleary, Larry Vorhis, Pete Mauthe and Heff Hershman.

in the first half. He was not alone in his embarrassment, because Pete Mauthe missed the extra-point attempt following McCleary's touchdown.

Pitt made several good gains in the second half but State's defense always tightened at the end.

In a rare display of editorial license normally reserved for the "home" team, if you will, the *Press* carried a related story on Nov. 26 under a banner headline which read, "VORHIS' MEN REJOICE." The story was a tribute to the Penn State seniors who had performed so admirably over the past four seasons.

Speculation at the time said that Pennsylvania and Lafayette were the top teams in the East. The *Press* gave its own vote of confidence to Penn State.

"Vorhis' warriors played their finest game of the year," according to the *Press* reporter. "A type of game that would have beaten either Penn or the Indians."

The story also said that undergraduates held a special reverence for McCleary, Tom Piolette and Vorhis. What follows is the *Press'* tribute to those players:

. . .Bull McCleary is the most benevolent looking fellow who has ever battled with a football opponent as he does on the gridiron. When McCleary starts to smile and shows you his big even rows of teeth, then you know that last year's captain is enjoying the conflict and is head-over-heels in the struggle. A Hercules in build, "Bull" is yet fast and a smooth sideline stepper; he can smash through on an off-tackle play as well as back up the line . . .

Seldom has Old State possessed a better end than Piolette. Last year he played much more than a mediocre game, yet it was far from the finished style he displayed this fall. "Shorty" must go down in State College history as one of Penn State's best ends for his work on forward passes, interference and getting down under punts . . .

Larry Vorhis, game to the core, square and fair in all his dealings, a clean cut athlete light in weight but wonderfully fast, a drop-kicker whose fame is no bigger than his playing merits . . .

It should be pointed out that the newspaper account was in error with regard to Tom Piolette, Penn State's end. He would not graduate for one more year and played in the 1910 game against Pitt.

1910

Game 13

Unbeaten and Unscored-upon

The way the series was progressing, Pitt was winning a game every so many years. You'd never guess how competitive some of these games actually were just by looking at the final ledger, which showed Penn State holding a 10-3 advantage through the first 13 games, including the 1910 contest. Yet in seven of these games, the winning margin was six points or less.

Backed by the running of Bill Hittner, and Huber Wagner, plus the quarterbacking of Herb Dewar, Norman Budd and Dave Richards, Pitt struggled to an 11-0 victory at Forbes Field in 1910. The Panthers also had a touchdown run by Budd called back on a holding penalty to Hittner, and Ralph Galvin missed field goals from 45 and 39 yards.

Richards wasted little time in forging Pitt to a 5-0 lead in the opening quarter by hurling a 42-yard pass to Hittner, who stutter-stepped his way past several Penn State defenders until Fritz Barrett brought him down on the Lion 8-yard line.

Two rushing plays followed, Richards and Dewar advancing the ball to the 1. Richards debated with his teammates what to call next, then decided to run the ball through the left side of the Panther line, behind the blocking of guard A. J. Blair and tackle George Bailey. A big hole opened up, which must have surprised Richards because he took his good ol' time going through it.

Pitt's Huber Wagner is about to tackle Penn State's Shorty Miller in the 1910 game.

Penn State rushed to close the gap and the resulting pileup left some doubt as to whether Richards crossed the goal line. Nevertheless, Pitt was awarded the touchdown but Galvin missed the PAT.

Penn State had an opportunity to tie the game in the second quarter. A bungled Pitt punt and four-yard Burley Watson-to-E. E. "Shorty" Miller pass placed the ball on the Lion 31-yard line. But Miller's next pass was intercepted by R. R. Feightner seconds before the half ended.

Both clubs changed quarterbacks in the second half, Pitt going with Dewar and Penn State reinserting Fred Johnson, who was injured early in the game.

Watson recovered a Pitt fumble near midfield at the quarter's end and had clear sailing ahead of him. But the lumbering giant slipped on some loose turf just over the 50. Penn State was forced to punt as the fourth quarter began.

Both teams exchanged punts, which seemed to comprise a vast majority of the action in this contest, and it was from a punt that the Panthers' final TD would result. Miller shanked one to his left from the Lion 45, and Huber Wagner, standing by his lonesome along the sidelines, cradled the ball and went unmolested 50 yards for a touchdown. Galvin's PAT made it 11-0.

Wagner's 50-yard score was the longest punt return TD of its kind in the early Pitt-Penn State matchups. The modern records are held by Penn State linebacker Dennis Onkotz, who ran one back 63 yards in 1968 and 71 yards in 1969.

However, neither of Onkotz' returns were scoring plays. So even though Wagner's touchdown is unrecognized in the record books, it today remains the longest punt return touchdown in Pitt-Penn State series history.

Pitt, incidentally, completed its first undefeated season (9-0) and became one of the select few in college football history to shut out its opponents along the way.

56

1911

Game 14

Hube

His name was Huber Wagner. Pitt players often referred to him simply as "Hube." Wagner was a two-way end when he played for the Panthers between 1910-13. The list of outstanding Pitt ends is impressive over the years . . . Joe Skladany, Mike Ditka, Jim Buckmon, Benjie Pryor, just to name a few.

But when you look back to Pitt's football origins, Huber Wagner's name stands out, especially in games played against Penn State. The man never failed to impress the audience of his day with his reckless tackling and romping ball-carrying ability.

Wagner was a defensive stalwart in the 1911 game despite being double-teamed by Bill Hollenback's Nittany Lions. Hube contributed his share of offensive firepower as well, with some memorable open-field running. But even his greatest individual effort fell short on Nov. 30, when Pete Mauthe booted a field goal (from an unspecified distance) to give Penn State a 3-0 victory at Forbes Field.

Afterward, Wagner blamed himself for the loss because he had failed to score a touchdown, even though Pitt botched three field goals on poor snaps.

"I just had the opportunities and few players overlook them on the gridiron," Wagner said. Speaking of overlooking something great, Wagner never made Walter Camp's All-America squad because Camp never saw Pitt play until 1915—two years after Wagner graduated.

Nonsense. Wagner was sensational. At one point in the contest he made seven unassisted tackles in succession before Bull Mc-Cleary, subbing as coach for Hollenback on this afternoon, ordered Wagner double-teamed on the line of scrimmage.

In the third quarter, Wagner intercepted a Shorty Miller pass and rambled 29 yards before Penn State's Dexter Very saved a game-

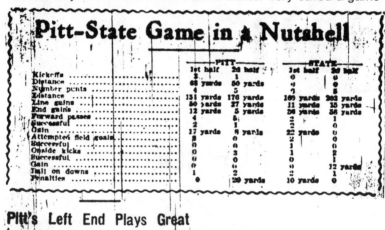

Pitt-State Game in a Nutshell

	PITT		STATE	
	1st half	2d half	1st half	2d half
Kickoffs	2	1	0	0
Distance	60 yards	60 yards	0	0
Number punts	4	5		
Distance	151 yards	176 yards	169 yards	203 yards
Line gains	50 yards	27 yards	11 yards	15 yards
End gains	12 yards	5 yards	36 yards	36 yards
Forward passes	4	5	2	1
Successful	2		2	0
Gain	17 yards	8 yards	22 yards	0
Attempted field goals	8	0	2	0
Successful	0	0	1	0
Onside kicks	0	3	1	2
Successful	0	0	0	
Gain	0	0	0	12 yards
Ball on downs	1	2	2	1
Penalties	0	20 yards	10 yards	0

Pitt's Left End Plays Great Game—Mauthe Makes a Bad Break When "Wag" Tears Off Long Run

Penn State team, 1911.

winning touchdown by hauling him down on the Lions' 36-yard line.

What no one seemed to realize in this moment of excitement was that Penn State had 12 men on the field. When it appeared that Wagner was going to score, Mauthe rushed off the bench and was about to tackle the Panther end. That's when Very appeared to make the play. The officials apparently never realized what Mauthe had done because no penalty was assessed.

The game dragged for most of the second half. The kicking stats seem to say much about each club's inability to move the football. Pitt kicked a total (kicks plus punts) of 327 yards while Penn State exceeded that by 45 yards. Only 11 forward passes had been attempted, a testament to an era in football when most teams preferred to keep the ball on the ground rather than risk losing it in the air.

Pitt Coach Joe Thompson had nothing but praise for Wagner. "Wagner's work was a revelation even to me," Thompson said, "and I think I know what he can do as well as any man in the world."

Thompson was not about to give Penn State any satisfaction in its victory, however.

"I am always willing to give a rival what is due," he said. "And I am willing to concede that State played great football, but I think the Centre County crowd was lucky to win. We played just as well as they did, and I fail to see where they have anything on Pitt in any department."

Thompson was obviously bothered by Pitt's 4-3-1 final record. Penn State finished 8-0-1, limiting its opposition to 15 points.

"We won because we deserved to win," said McCleary in Hollenback's absence. "We had the better team and I never had any doubt about the outcome. Pitt played good ball, and I am willing to concede that they gave us the hardest fight we have had this season. It was a glorious victory."

1912

Game 15

A 20-Point Effort

Fullback Pete Mauthe had been a hero the year before with a game-winning field goal over Pitt. Little did Mauthe realize then, but in 1912 he would personally account for 20 points while booting a series-record 51-yard field goal that has withstood challenge since, including Chris Bahr's 50-yarder against Pitt in 1974.

Mauthe scored two touchdowns and was five-for-five in PATs as Penn State romped to a 38-0 victory at Forbes Field. The win completed the Lions' perfect 8-0 season, one in which they gave up just six points (to Cornell).

Pitt finished a miserable 3-6. Coach Joe Thompson, after guiding the Panthers to a 9-0 record in 1910, was replaced by Joseph Duff following this game. Thompson, unfortunately, had won just seven games during his last two years at the school.

Penn State opened up a 17-0 lead on Pitt in the first half as Mauthe booted his famous field goal and added two touchdowns. Pitt, which had trouble blocking and tackling throughout the season, actually improved upon those facets of play in this game, or so it was written in one newspaper account.

Pitt's best chance to ruin State's shutout came in the final quarter when the Panthers drove downfield for three consecutive first downs to the Lions' 15-yard line. Huber Wagner attempted a field goal from there but the kick was wide of the uprights.

Penn State Hall of Fame members, from left, Shorty Miller, Pete Mauthe and Dexter Very.

Punk Berryman, Penn State fullback, 1912.

HOW STATE WON
CONTEST FROM
PITT TEAM

Mauthe, Very and Miller
Lead in Game at Forbes
Field.

VICTORY IS CLEAN-CUT

Before it was over, quarterback Shorty Miller, end Capt. Dexter Very, and halfback Punk Berryman would add touchdowns for Penn State while Mauthe tried his hand at quarterback and completed several passes. It's interesting that both the *Pittsburgh Post-Gazette* and *Press* often referred to Berryman as "Merryman" in their story.

To a degree, both papers were right about one thing. The Penn State 11, having buried Pitt 38-0, were indeed Merry Men.

Footnote: Because early newspaper stories sometimes referred to laterals as passes and pitches as the same, it is hard to pinpoint when the first scoring pass occurred in this series. The forward pass was introduced in 1906. Although both clubs threw it often, Pete Mauthe's 32-yard strike to Dexter Very in this game is *believed* to be the first scoring pass in the series.

1913

Game 16

Hide the Check

The headlines announced how Pitt's first season under Joseph Duff had ended "gloriously." Duff's Panthers defeated Penn State, 7-6 at Forbes Field to close the season with a 6-2-1 mark.

"Pitt's Fine Victory Over Penn State Pleases Local Followers in Great American College Pastime," the *Pittsburgh Press* declared just above the bylined story of Ralph S. Davis.

The game held special significance for both teams. Pitt's two-way end, Huber Wagner, and Penn State quarterback Shorty Miller were making their last appearances in college uniforms. Both received ovations from the crowd following the game. Wagner was also treated to a dinner by his teammates and presented with a $100 check, which today would invoke all sorts of nasty complications (probably in the form of probation) by the NCAA. Back then, college football was largely unregulated as Big Brother hadn't yet asserted itself on the nation's institutions of higher learning.

Like so many games between these two clubs, this was another one of those battles in the trenches, trite as it may sound. All the scoring was done in the second quarter. Penn State cracked the ice with John Clark's rushing touchdown, but Miller missed the PAT. That blunder would prove fatal to the Lions at the end.

Pitt tied the game 6-6 later that quarter on a bulldozing 67-yard scoring run by G. M. Williamson. Williamson added his own PAT for the 7-6 difference.

Shorty Miller, Penn State quarterback, 1913.

Penn State mounted several drives at the end, one deep into Pitt territory, but costly penalties kept the Lions from sustaining them. Penn State's last drive was halted by the final whistle.

Pitt fans declared their Panthers as true state champions after the game. The debate raged even in the Pittsburgh newspapers. William & Jefferson thought it should be Number One because it had defeated Penn State, 17-0, and Pitt, 18-6.

Back East, the Philadelphia newspapers were hailing Penn (who else?) as state champions. Ralph S. Davis' column in the *Press* on Nov. 28 summed up the entire situation this way:

Philadelphia now knows where it belongs in the football class. Old Penn's defeat by Cornell yesterday was one of the many big surprises of the season and shows rather the weakness of the Quakers than the strength of the Ithacans. It is a very hard matter for residents of Philadelphia to see any team in the country except Penn . . .

If there is a better football team in the country than W&J, it is hard to pick. The immense score piled up against Bucknell yesterday shows that the Red and Black men played their string out and never let up for an instant during the season. Shorty Miller, of State, says Wash-Jeff has the best aggregation of gridders he ever saw—and Shorty has lamped a few luminaries in his day. W&J claims the collegiate title of Pennsylvania—and has a perfect right to do so.

Ralph Davis would write many excellent football columns for the *Press*. The above excerpts were taken from a "notes" column he penned that day. In it, Davis raised the question whether it wouldn't be more exciting for Pitt and Penn State to play "under the lamplights."

Davis would never see it happen, but night football between these two teams would someday become a reality.

1914

Game 17

Two in a Row!

Two positions in football that are worthy of mention, but seldom enjoy such, are that of center and middle guard. Everyone takes for granted the routine motion which comes with snapping a football or plugging a hole and making the tackle. Such are the respective duties of center and middle guard, in their most simple form.

Bob Peck played both positions for the Panthers from 1914 until his graduation in 1916. In 1914, he became Pitt's first football All-American and in 1954 would be honored as the school's first Hall of Fame inductee.

Although Sandy Hastings kicked two field goals to ensure Pitt's 13-3 victory in 1914, it was Peck who distinguished himself at Forbes Field. In the words of football writer Ralph S. Davis of the *Pittsburgh Press*, "Peck was not glued to any one spot, but moved about with the speed of a backfield man, being in practically every play, and doing much toward checking the State advances."

The victory marked the first time in the series that Pitt had won back-to-back games. To give you an idea of the importance placed on this game, consider that Capt. Todd of State played despite suffering severe burns in a fiery explosion following a team celebration after the Harvard game. Todd played, according to the *Press*, "swathed in bandages"—an all-white mummy on a football field of Blue & Gold and Blue & White. It was a gutty performance by Todd during a season when the 5-3-1 Lions were in no position to capture post-season honors.

Following a scoreless first half, Hastings drop-kicked a 34-yard field goal giving Pitt a 3-0 lead. By the third quarter's end, Pitt had stretched the lead to 10-0 on a touchdown run by Mr. Collins, first name unknown, and Hasting's PAT.

Penn State mounted its only scoring drive in the fourth quarter but settled on Levi Lamb's 30-yard field goal when several rushes failed to produce a first down. Minutes later, Hastings added his final field goal, this one from 28 yards, making the final score 13-3.

Though this game was played in late November, the weather was unseasonably warm and by game's end, several Penn State players were laid out along the sideline suffering from heat exhaustion.

The Panthers (8-1) outrushed the Lions, 157-101 in yards. Punting yardage was phenomenal. Pitt racked up 366 yards to Penn State's 316, although neither team had more than 44 yards in punt-return yardage.

Lion Coach Bill Hollenback left the Mt. Nittany scene following this game as did Panther boss Joe Duff, who had won 14 games, lost three and tied one in two seasons. Duff would be replaced at Pitt by Glenn Scobey "Pop" Warner, who was destined to become a legend in his own time.

1915

Game 18

Pop Warner Football

Pop Warner's first season in Pittsburgh had been a triumphant success. The Panthers' 20-0 win over Penn State at Forbes Field wrapped up an 8-0 season. In the days that followed, Pitt would be voted National Champions for the first time in school history.

Warner's debut against State proved to be a memorable occasion as the game was virtually full of electrifying runs by the Panthers. Sandy Hastings, Pitt's left halfback, rambled for two touchdowns, kicked a field goal and added his own PATs. His 17 points overshadowed the running of G. M. Williamson, who returned one kickoff 50 yards, then followed up that play with a 40-yard touchdown run. Panther reserve quarterback James DeHart, however, was credited with the game's best run. DeHart returned a punt 60 yards.

Indeed, this was one Pitt club with an abundance of running talent at all positions. Penn State rookie coach Dick Harlow was inclined to agree.

"I think," Harlow said, "we were beaten by the best team in the land today."

Perhaps one reason Pitt played so well in this game was Williamson's workload had been cut in half by Warner prior to the contest. In past games, Williamson had been calling the offensive signals.

Pitt averted early embarrassment after Williamson fumbled away a pass on the opening kickoff at his own 6-yard line. Four times Penn State rushed into the seam of the Pitt line but failed to produce

In
Whom
We
Trust

GLENN S. WARNER
Coach-Elect

Glenn S. "Pop" Warner, Pitt Head Coach, 1915 to 1923.

Pitt Entitled to Dispute Cornell's Claim to the 1915 Football Honors

Victory Over Penn State In Annual Game Places Gold and Blue Around Top—Hastings Is One of the Stars of the Contest.

LOCALS SHOW A POWERFUL ATTACK

a touchdown. The Panthers' goal line stand inspired the offense. By the first quarters' end, Pitt held a 10-0 lead.

Hastings, Williamson and George McLaren, who would play most of the contest with a broken arm, though he didn't realize it, combined efforts for 45 yards as the Panthers drove to the Lion 26 late in the quarter. Following a three-yard loss by Hastings, the latter elected to kick a field goal for a 3-0 edge.

That set up Williamson's 50-yard return and subsequent 40-yard touchdown run and PAT giving Pitt its 10-0 advantage.

Penn State soon came to the realization that running the ball was futile against Pitt's huge linemen. An assortment of odd formations and passes occurred in the second quarter, including a triple pass, believed to be the first ever attempted in this series, from Stan Ewing-to-Harold Clark-to-Chuck Yerger-to-Ewing. A Pitt player broke up the final leg of the completion on the Panther 5-yard line. Undaunted, Penn State came right back with a double pass involving Clark and Ewing, but the drive stalled out inside the 5.

An early third-quarter drive by Penn State was washed out at the Panther 11 when Clark slipped going around end, botching an apparent touchdown. The Lions attempted a field goal from there, but Clark's kick hit the uprights. Nothing was going right for Penn State.

An exchange of punts saw Penn State regain the ball. Very methodically Penn State moved the ball upfield with fancy passes mixed in with occasional runs. Again, fate dealt the Lions a severe blow. Ewing's pass on the Panther 23 was intercepted by McLaren at the 17, thus killing another potential State rally.

Penn State turned the ball over again on an interception minutes later, which fueled Pitt on its way to scoring its final touchdown of the afternoon, this one, a 27-yard run by Hastings, making it 17-0.

Pitt added a 13-yard field goal by R. A. Gougler seconds before the final gun.

Pop Warner sought out each Panther to offer his congratulations. Pitt had won its third game in a row over Penn State. Warner would win five more times against his rival, tie twice and lose just once.

1916
Game 19

An Innovator, Too

Glenn "Pop" Warner's contribution to football is a matter of record. What he was accomplishing at Pitt would leave indelible marks on the game. Warner would ultimately be judged among the ranks of Notre Dame's Knute Rockne and Chicago's Amos Alonzo Stagg because of the single and double wing formations he deployed.

What few people seem to remember, however, was Warner's other innovation. The one that came in 1916 and would make the game easier to follow for fans, writers and broadcasters.

Warner's idea was so simple it seems absurd to think that no one thought of it sooner. His brainstorm: to place numbers on jerseys for easy identification.

Besides walloping Penn State 31-0 in 1916, Pitt became the first team to wear uniform numbers. The rest of the country wasn't far behind in adopting Warner's suggestion.

Reporters at the time were so caught up with the fact that Warner's club had just clinched its second straight National Championship that they forgot to mention how Pitt blew apart Penn State in the game. Instead, they chose to bestow a mountain of accolades on Warner, Sandy Hastings and Bob Peck.

It is known Hastings scored at least one touchdown at Forbes Field, added his own PAT and booted two field goals. Pitt scored nine points in the opening quarter, 15 in the second and seven in the third. It was the worst drubbing Penn State had suffered since a 22-5 loss to Pitt in 1904.

Hastings, who was later named to the All-America squad, had the

Sandy Hastings, Pitt halfback. He scored seven points against Penn State in 1914, 17 in 1915 and 13 in 1916.

Pitt's second National Championship squad, 1916.

BOB PECK AND "POP" WARNER—1916

longest touchdown run of the day, 75 yards off a lateral by George McLaren, a future Panther Hall of Famer.

Umpire Robert W. Maxwell, whose guest column appeared in the *Pittsburgh Press* on Dec. 1, claimed Peck had played his greatest game as the Panthers' center and middle guard. In justifying this claim, Maxwell pointed out that Peck had suffered a severe blow to the head early in the game, yet refused to sit down.

Peck's injury slowed the Panthers in the first half because quarterback James DeHart was forced to explain every call to Peck *before* shouting the signals over center.

There was much debate afterward as to whether Pitt, Army or Brown would stake claim to the National Championship. Brown's 28-0 loss to Colgate solved part of the problem, but that still left Pitt and Army.

Maxwell's argument for Pitt centered primarily on Warner's coaching ability. "There is no doubt about Pittsburgh's claim to the championship," Maxwell wrote. "In fact, they don't even have to claim it. It will be handed out to the men who were taught the game by Glenn Warner, on a silver platter, regardless of the howls emanating from West Point for recognition. Pitt has many arguments to back her claim, the first being a clean slate for two years, and the other arguments can be forgotten after that."

Pitt had again gone undefeated (8-0) and beaten a Penn State squad (8-2) that had not given up 31 points to one opponent in 15 years! Maxwell reiterated his contention that Warner was a special kind of collegiate mentor.

". . . Warner is the greatest coach that ever had charge of a football team," he wrote. "This statement is not due to excessive enthusiasm, or anything like that. It comes after a close study of the coaching methods of the leading gridiron tutors of the country in the past 10 years."

Maxwell went so far as to say that Warner was "in a class by himself and outshines . . . Alonzo Stagg." Some Chicagoans regarded that last statement as downright blasphemy.

Another special honor given the Panthers was the selection of center Bob Peck to the All-America squad. It was Peck's third consecutive appearance on the team. In years to come, only running back Tony Dorsett, a four-time All-American, and defensive end Hugh Green (three times) would garner as much recognition.

A final word about Peck. He was a passing center who led Warner's famous single and double wing attack, which was then in its infancy.

1917

Game 20

25th Straight Win

Pitt completed its third successive unbeaten season with a 28-6 victory over Penn State at Forbes Field upon a slippery, muddy turf that didn't appear to bother the Panthers very much.

Pop Warner's Panthers had won their 25th straight game without defeat to be ranked No. 1 in the East with a 9-0 record. Three Panthers were later named All-Americans—tackle H. C. Carlson, and guards Jock Sutherland and Dale Sies.

R. A. Gougler, the man who put the finishing touches on a 20-0 win over State two years earlier with a field goal, accounted for 17 points in this game with two touchdowns and three extra points. Fullback George McLaren and halfback H. C. McCarter each tallied once.

Former Penn State Coach Bill Hollenback, who had stepped down following the 1913 season, was permitted to officiate this game, even though such a move was viewed with some skepticism by the media and Pitt officials.

Legend has it that Warner allowed Hollenback to officiate as a gesture of good faith. Hollenback had coached three Penn State teams to undefeated seasons—1909, 1911 and 1912. He took a year off in 1910 to coach Missouri while his brother, Jack, struggled to a 5-2-1 season on Mt. Nittany. Warner, it is said, was deeply impressed with Hollenback's brief stint at State. Thus, Warner allowed him to work the game.

Pitt scored twice in the opening quarter to take a 14-0 lead but Penn State, using a spread formation devised by Lion assistant coach Ken Scott, answered with a touchdown of its own in the second quarter, cutting the deficit to 14-6.

R. A. Gougler, Pitt halfback, 1917.

Warner's troops seemed confused by Penn State's formations, in which the backfield lined up directly behind the ends and the center, positioned sideways, snapped to one of the backs. Such a formation, of course, would be ruled illegal under today's rules. But Lion Coach Dick Harlow allowed Scott to experiment with these formations provided they achieved results. And they did, as quarterback Charley Way hurled a tacky triple touchdown pass to Larry Conover for the Lions' only score of the afternoon. The pass went from center Red Griffiths to Red Gross, from Gross to Harry Robb, Robb to Charlie Way and finally, Way to Conover. The play covered 20 yards.

During the halftime intermission, Warner concocted a defense to prevent Penn State from inflicting further damage with its spread attack, while Pitt scored two more times, making the final score 28-6.

Rutgers Coach Foster Stanford, who watched from the stands, remarked after the game that he had gained valuable insight into Pitt's downfield blocking schemes. Stanford contended that Warner was a genius when it came to designing plays that protected the ballcarrier.

"Glenn Warner has such a wonderful attack, and I don't see how it can be stopped," Stanford said. "I imagined from what I had read that the man with the ball could be tackled from behind, but there are too many interferers around him . . . Warner seems to be the only man who can teach it."

Two days after having swept Penn State under the rug, Pitt defeated a military contingent from Camp Lee in an exhibition game.

This was Harlow's last season but never let it be said he didn't leave a lasting impression on Penn State. As a dorm proctor, he allowed the students to settle disputes with boxing matches. Thus began boxing as an intercollegiate sport at Penn State in 1919. Naturally, Harlow coached the team.

It is said that he scouted (spied) Pitt one year and was discovered by a bunch of unruly players who attempted to pry his notebook. A fight ensued as Harlow decked the leader, sending him 10 flights down the stands, then scaled the fence, jumping 20 feet to safety. Harlow's legendary feats would be topped by his successor, Hugo Bezdek.

• • •

After 20 games, Penn State led the series in victories with 12, while Pitt had eight. The Lions badly outscored the Panthers over that stretch, 256-148.

1918

Game 21

Hugo Bezdek

The season had been cut in half because of World War I, but by the time Pitt and Penn State met on Nov. 28, there was reason to celebrate.

President Woodrow Wilson drew up his famed "Fourteen Points" for peace in the early part of the month and on Nov. 11, Germany had signed the armistice. The real battle was over.

Back home, Pitt continued its mastery over Penn State winning by the same margin as the season before, 28-6, at Forbes Field, as fullback George McLaren ran for three touchdowns to spoil Penn State Coach Hugo Bezdek's introduction to Pitt-PSU football.

Bezdek's boys actually led in this affair, 6-0, in the opening minutes of play, aided by the running of Glenn Killinger, who helped State advance the ball inside the Panther 10. The Lions actually got most of their yardage on a gift when R. A. Gougler muffed a punt that died at the Pitt 19.

Once inside the Pitt 10, Frank Unger ran around end for Penn State's only score in the game. Red Henry's extra point sailed wide of its mark so, the score stood at 6-0.

Pitt forged ahead on the ensuing kickoff. The drive was highlighted by halfback Tom Davies, 40-yard burst and George McLaren's 13-yard run, placing the ball on the Lion 7-yard line. Davies advanced it to the 5, setting up McLaren's first touchdown. Davies' PAT gave Pitt a 7-6 edge.

Hugo Bezdek, Penn State Head Coach, 1918 to 1929.

Davies hurled a 25-yard pass to McLaren late in the second quarter setting up Pitt's next score from the Lion 5-yard line. Again, it was the big fullback going over with Davies kicking the extra point. Pitt was in the driver's seat, 14-6.

A costly Lion fumble at their 22 in the third quarter was responsible for Pitt's next score. On first down, Davies ran around end, McLaren completed a pass there, and Pitt led 21-6 following the point-after.

McLaren racked up 38 more yards during Pitt's next drive, which culminated with his final TD of the day, making it 28-6. Both teams fumbled in each other's territory in the fourth quarter, but such miscues hurt Penn State more because it never quite got untracked in this game.

The Lions' attack was so dreadful that Bezdek figured he'd surprise Pitt by quick-kicking on first down late in the game. Even that backfired, as Unger's boot groaned its way to the State's 45-yard line. The game mercifully ended with Pitt threatening to score from the Penn State 22.

Davies and McLaren were named All-Americans while Pitt (4-0) was once again hailed as National Champions. The generally accepted system of determining a national champion—namely, the wire service polls—would not emerge until 1924.

As for Hugo Bezdek, his first season on Mt. Nittany was a 1-2-1 sled ride, but things were destined to improve for the former All-American from Chicago. His Lions would lose only one game over the next three seasons.

Penn State coaching staff. From left, Newsh Bentz, Larry Conover, Hugo Bezdek, Dutch Herman and Bas Gray.

Bezdek is one of the fascinating characters of the early 1900s. His sporting interests exceeded college football. From 1917 to 1919, Hugo would drive from State College to Pittsburgh once the football season ended. Upon arriving in the Steel City, he would don the manager's cap of the Pirates. His 1919 Pirates won the World Series. Bezdek bowed out of baseball as a champion shortly after.

He was later elected to the Penn State Hall of Fame, National Football Hall of Fame, and Helms Foundation College Football Hall of Fame.

Speaking of fame, in 1965, Pitt enshrined George McLaren, who is considered the school's greatest fullback. During his four years (1915-18), Pitt was 29-0. In 1917, he rushed for 782 yards, a record no other Panther fullback has bettered. But McLaren's claim to fame is this: He was never stopped without making a gain during his entire collegiate career.

1919

Game 22

Daring the Odds

Twenty points.

Beginning in 1919 and lasting for a full three years, that's all the points which would be scored in the annual Pitt-Penn State battle. Unfortunately for Pop Warner, all 20 points would be scored by Penn State in this one game.

The contest featured some outstanding plays, including the game-buster in the first quarter. Recall that Lion Coach Hugo Bezdek had tried to fool Warner the year before with a quick kick on first down. Pitt, however, was ready and the play backfired.

This time, Bezdek's unorthodox play-calling worked. The Panthers had pushed Penn State back to its own 5-yard line. On fourth down, the Lions lined up in punt formation with fullback Harold Hess, the supposed punter, standing in the end zone awaiting the snap.

But when Hess got the ball, he rushed forward and fired a pass to his end, Bob Higgins. Higgins galloped a series-record 75 yards for a touchdown and a 6-0 lead. The crowd at Forbes Field was stunned by the daring call, but as football historians later noted, what made the Pitt-Penn State matchup such a classic football rivalry from 1919 through the mid-20s was the hell-bent, damn the odds type of football strategy practiced by Bezdek and Warner.

Following the 20-0 victory, *Pittsburgh Press* sportswriter Ralph S. Davis accurately captured the Panthers' feelings in this game when

Bob Higgins, Penn State All-American, 1919.

he wrote, "Playing a wonderful brand of football, mixing things up in a manner that completely bewildered their opponents, they (Penn State) took the proud Warnerites into camp in the most decisive fashion, the game never being in doubt after the first few minutes."

Penn State widened its lead to 13-0 on a touchdown by Hess in the second quarter. The Lions racked up eight first downs (Pitt had none) and ran every direction at Pitt. Charley Way, the Lions' speedy little halfback, zig-zagged up and down the field time and again with punts of 25 and 30 yards. Then he and Hess would grind out another first down.

Following Hess' score, Way scampered 45 yards for a touchdown on a third-and-short yardage situation in the third quarter. Way broke through a stack of players for his final score, then outran Pitt's Sandy Hastings, who had returned to school after serving his country in WW I.

So decisive was Penn State's victory, that Pitt failed to complete a single pass. Penn State outgained Pitt in yards, too, 288-110.

Despite the loss, spectators left Forbes Field marveling about the unusual plays they had seen and how keen a football mind Hugo Bezdek had to pull such stunts on Warner.

"It can be said there was no bitterness over the defeat on Pitt's part," the *Press* reported. "It had drunk heartily from the cup of victory at State's expense in seasons past, and it was ready and willing to drain the cup of defeat without even a grimace."

Pitt halfback Tom Davies was selected to the All-America team and in 1970, Davies entered the Panther Hall of Fame. Penn State's Bob Higgins celebrated his senior year by becoming the Lions' second All-American. He was enshrined in the Penn State Hall of Fame, where he joined such early 1900 members as quarterback Glenn Killinger, fullback/kicker Pete Mauthe and quarterback Shorty Miller.

1920

Game 23

0-0

Their faces were similar in structure. Round with a broad, square chin. They wore the look of seriousness, Pop Warner and Hugo Bezdek. They were intense, fearless competitors. Above all, Warner and Bezdek were gambling men.

You could almost picture them as a pair of card counters on the Mississippi Queen. Get these two guys in a poker game and the house would fold.

They lived dangerously on the football field. Why kick a field goal when you can score six points, they reasoned. Besides, there is nothing honorable in taking the easy way out with a field goal. True men went right at each other. Lineman to lineman. Let the running backs decide an affair, not a kicker.

Such boldness or stubbornness, depending upon your point of view, hurt both coaches in the 1920 game. The final score was 0-0, but as we shall see, a tie could have been easily averted if either coach had played a safe hand instead of holding out for aces.

It's difficult to say which team or players felt worse after the game. Penn State quarterback Glenn Killinger fumbled twice deep inside Panther territory and was yanked at the end in favor of Tom Ritner. Pitt's quarterback, Herb Stein, didn't fare much better. He threw a bad pass at the beginning of the third quarter—on fourth down, no less—with Pitt nestled on State's 4-yard line.

Pitt had a golden opportunity to score in the first half but Tom

Penn State Varsity, 1920.

Davies coughed up the ball on Penn State's 20. Charley Way recovered for the Lions but on first down, Killinger fumbled it back to Pitt. The Panthers drove to the 8 before Penn State's defense refused to move any farther.

For reasons known only to him, Warner elected to rush for the first down from the Lion 4 instead of attempting a field goal. That mistake would occur again in the third quarter when Pitt tried a pass instead of kicking a field goal.

Penn State did the same thing in the third quarter. Four times Killinger attempted to gnaw his way to the goal line from the Pitt 10 and four times he was rebuffed. Bezdek wouldn't hear of trying a field goal. After all, Warner had dared the odds and now Pop was calling his bluff. Rather than fold, Bezdek played his own card. Except neither man won the hand.

Minutes later, in the fourth quarter, Penn State got the ball back after a poor Panther punt rolled harmlessly to the Pitt 45. Way and

Killinger moved the ball to 15. Now Bezdek was facing another fourth down; this time, his Lions needed two yards. Again, Bezdek ignored the logic of kicking a field goal. Instead, he instructed Way to run the ball around left end. Trouble was, Warner anticipated that play and had John McClean waiting there. McClean threw Way for a three-yard loss.

Imagine the frustration and bewilderment of those who watched this game at Forbes Field.

Considering the intensity with which Warner and Bezdek coached against each other, perhaps fans came to expect such. Of the two, Bezdek was the more temperamental. His players hated him, although some like Frank Diedrich worked harder because of him. He openly warred with his team and once told them he wanted men who gave "something better" than their best, whatever that was. When he managed the Pirates, Bezdek used to engage in fisticuffs. After one such tete-a-tete with Pirate pitcher Burleigh Grimes on a Pullman car traveling New York-to-Pittsburgh, Bezdek shouted at him, "You'll still pitch tomorrow!"

Hugh Bezdek was one rough sumbitch.

Bezdek's reputation as a brawler began in his college days at Chicago, where he played football under Amos Alonzo Stagg. Hugo honed his boxing skills on the side. Rumors were, he was being paid. When Stagg inquired about this he was told by Morgan Athletic Club President Frank Ragan, "Hugo fought for the love of the game. But I paid him $75."

His love for the brute within us all came through in his coaching days at Penn State. He drove his players with a conviction that if only he could break them, surely, no opponent could. Tuesday practices were called "Bloody Tuesday" because of numerous player scuffles.

Hugo left a lasting impression on everyone. Especially Pop Warner. The dislike for Warner was so strong, Bezdek used to pull the players' bench onto the field to disrupt play and rattle Warner. Warner outfoxed him by having the Forbes Field benches staked to the ground.

1921

Game 24

Perry's Purple Prose

Among the many bylined reporters who covered the Pitt-Penn State affair through the years, the *Philadelphia Inquirer's* Perry Lewis far outdistanced his nearest peer when it came to "purple prose" journalism.

Perry's typewriter dripped with flowery description, cliche writing and unintentional humor. Every game was an adventure, not a story.

Ralph S. Davis had distinguished himself at the *Pittsburgh Press* because he was, above anything else, a fair-minded reporter whose style was not that far off from many of today's sportswriters.

Lewis, however, was the sensational breed of reporter whose writing skills only a William Randolph Hearst could have appreciated. Too bad for Lewis that a racy tabloid known as the *Philadelphia Daily News* would not come to be until 1925. It was the perfect vehicle for Lewis' writing style.

Penn State and Pitt battled to another 0-0 tie in 1921. Perry Lewis attempted to collar the flavor of the game in the opening two paragraphs of his story:

PITTSBURGH, Pa., Nov. 24—The lion of Nittany Mountain, roving the country, seeking whom it might devour, stalked into the rain-soaked lair of the Panther of Pater Pitt this Thanksgiving Day. As the king of beasts roared its defiance to the football world, the feline of "Pop" Warner hurled itself upon the invader. In a sea of mud the monarchs of the jungle snarled, tore and ripped at each other, and at the end of an hour of furious action neither had been able to overcome the other.

Penn State was unable to score, and so was Pitt, but that grim battle, fought in mire ankle deep, will never be forgotten by the 34,000 football-mad fans who braved the elements to seek a seat in the jammed stands.

Like the year before, both teams, despite the awful rain, had a chance to win this game. And once again, Pop Warner and Hugo Bezdek ignored field goal attempts in favor of running the ball, even passing it at the most inopportune moments.

Running the ball, however, made little difference in this game because both teams' most potent weapons—Penn State quarterback Glenn Killinger and Pitt halfback Tom Davies—were powerless to do anything on Forbes Field's mud-slick turf.

The Lions' first real opportunity came in the second quarter when Killinger punted to Davies. Davies misplayed the ball, hoping it would bounce into the end zone, but, in the words of Perry Lewis, "a perverse imp of fate" caused the ball to squirt to the Pitt 5-yard line. Davies wasn't thinking very clearly at this point and attempted to scoop the ball up and run.

He was hit at the Pitt 12 and fumbled, State's Harry "Light Horse" Wilson recovering the ball. Wilson nullified his own good play moments later with a fumble of his own. Pitt failed to capitalize on this stroke of good fortune because Davies immediately fumbled the ball away at the Panther 17.

According to Lewis, ". . . Wilson and (Joe) Lightner, those two great plunging backs, smote the Pitt line with deadly venom, only to feel it bend but not break." As a last resort, Killinger threw on fourth down, but middle guard Herb Stein batted the ball down at the Panther 5 as "four grimy State hands clutched for it."

Lewis wrote that Pitt was better prepared in the second half and speculated "Glenn Warner must have fed the Panthers more raw meat between the halves . . ."

Lightner opened the second half with a fumble and Pitt recovered at the Lion 40. Fullback Lewis Colonna ate up the yardage as Pitt drove to the Penn State three-yard line. That's as far as the Panthers went. Davies tried a forward pass of his own and Wilson picked it off.

Pitt had one last chance to win the game in the fourth quarter deep in Lion territory, but Davies again was intercepted. Incidentally, in case you're wondering, it was Davies, not quarterback Tom Holleran, who twice threw the ball on key downs and twice was intercepted.

Penn State returned home to State College with an 8-0-2 record, still the Beast of the East.

Perry Lewis summed things up this way:

And in this desperate fray Pitt won because she did not lose and State lost because she did not win.

1922

Game 25

Finally, Some Points

Pitt finally ended its three-year scoring drought with a 14-0 victory over Penn State that enabled the Panthers to close out their season with an 8-2 record.

Halfbacks John Anderson and Hoot Flanagan and fullback Tiny Hewitt were the battering rams that pounded Penn State's line most of the afternoon.

The first half ended 0-0, thus prolonging the scoreless string of quarters to 10 (from 1920) in this famed rivalry. Flanagan gave Pitt its first points since 1918 in the third quarter with a one-yard burst over tackle, then plowed smack into the goal post, nearly knocking himself unconscious.

Flanagan set up the touchdown himself with a brilliant 44-yard punt return to the Lion 16-yard line. He then rammed it to the 1 on consecutive tries up the middle.

Pitt's early 7-0 lead followed an unsuccessful 34-yard field goal attempt by the Panthers' Harold Williams.

Pitt got an insurance touchdown in the fourth quarter on a 15-yard Flanagan-to-Anderson touchdown pass. The drive began at the Panther 34 with Hewitt bulldozing his way through the Penn State line, churning out 41 yards on repeated carries till the weary fullback gave way to Lewis Colonna at the Lion 25. State's line tightened for one down, then Colonna pushed his way to the 15, leaving it up to Flanagan and Anderson.

PITT TEARS THROUGH STATE AND WINS, 14-0, IN ANNUAL GRID TEST

Hoot Flanagan, Penn State halfback, 1922.

At no time in this game did Penn State threaten to score. What made the loss even more bitter for Hugo Bezdek to accept was that Penn State was headed for the Rose Bowl to play Southern Cal despite its 6-3-1 season slate.

If you're wondering how the Lions were able to secure a bowl bid in 1922 with such a poor record when they had gone undefeated in two previous seasons without invitation, the answer is, the bowl trip had all been pre-planned.

As early as three months *before* the 1922 season, Penn State officials decided to accept the Rose Bowl's bid, provided a satisfactory opponent could be found. The Rose Bowl desperately wanted Penn State.

Bezdek's 1921 squad had gone 8-0-2 but had not played Washington & Jefferson, which defeated Pitt, 7-0. Recall that Pitt and Penn State wrestled to a 0-0 tie. Rose Bowl officials were divided over whether to pick Penn State or W&J for their game against California that year. As it was, they chose W&J, which battled Cal to a 0-0 tie.

Of course, not even the Rose Bowl people foresaw Penn State losing to Navy, Penn and Pitt in 1922, not to mention tying Syracuse, 0-0.

They had been impressed with Bezdek's past performances and were willing to risk signing Penn State prior to the season, foolish as it may sound.

Furthermore, bowl officials were well aware that Penn State hadn't lost in two years. Plus, Bezdek had become sort of a legend on the West Coast, where he coached at Oregon between 1913-17. His 1917 team shut out nationally-touted Penn, 14-0 in the Rose Bowl.

It is said Bezdek intentionally delayed the start of the 1923 game 45 minutes, claiming his team was held up in Rose Bowl parade traffic. Why the subterfuge? Bezdek and USC Coach Elmer "Gloomy Gus" Henderson were bitter rivals during Bezdek's Oregon trail days.

In any event, it was Bezdek who wore the look of gloom on New Year's Day after USC upended Penn State, 14-3.

• • •

The 1922 encounter marked the 25th game played between Pitt and Penn State. The series: Penn State 13, Pittsburgh 10, 2 ties. Penn State had outscored Pitt, 292-190.

1923

Game 26

Pop Gives Way
to Jock

After nine seasons at the Panther helm, this game was to mark Pop Warner's exit from Pitt football. During Warner's stay he had directed the Panther's to three National Championships while compiling a 59-11-4 record.

It would be nice to say that Pop Warner finished his career at Pitt having gone undefeated with another title. Such is the stuff by which legends are made. Nice perhaps, but not true. Pitt had a dismal 5-4 record in '23. That didn't matter much, though, because the Panthers had won the big one, the one that *really* counted. On Thanksgiving Day, they lanced Penn State, 20-3 at Forbes Field before 35,000. Pop Warner had gone out a winner.

A new name surfaced in this series. Karl Bohren, Pitt's lithe halfback, made his presence known to all with a 70-yard touchdown in the second quarter. He also hurled a 15-yard scoring pass to Hoot Flanagan earlier that quarter as Pitt broke in front 14-0.

That series saw the Panthers drive 71 yards with Flanagan and Bohren, nicknamed "Jakey," alternating passes between themselves. Quarterback Rick Shuler must have felt somewhat left out of the play. In the early days, backs were seen throwing the football simply because the coaching philosophy then was to allow your best athlete, usually a running back, to throw the ball. In time, the

Thanksgiving Day, 1923 at Forbes Field: Pitt halfback Karl Bohren lofts a 15-yard touchdown pass to Hoot Flanagan.

best athlete would be any number of people on a squad, but the role of play-calling and throwing would be left to the man standing directly behind center.

Pitt scored again in the third quarter off a Lion turnover. Penn State kicker Hobie Light took too much time in getting his end zone punt away, thus allowing Panther end Milo Gwosden to charge across the goal line and block the punt. Gwosden fell on the ball for an easy six points. That made it 20-3, Penn State's only points having come in the first quarter on Dick Schuster's field goal.

Pitt played another spectacular defensive game, holding Penn State to just two first downs. Indeed, it was a terribly frustrating afternoon for Lion halfback Harry "Light Horse" Wilson, an All-American in 1923.

Wilson had received ample notoriety resulting from his stalwart running efforts on mud two years earlier in a 0-0 tie. The pre-game buildup centered on Wilson's forte as a game-breaker.

Light Horse may have been the most exciting running back in Penn State history and had the distinction of being the leading scorer for two years at two different schools — Penn State (1922-23) and Army (1925-26).

But for this game, Pop Warner had designed a defense to seal off Wilson's elusive runs around the end. Few people really appreciated the genius of Warner, who would devise a defense, make an adjustment here and there, all to stop the opposing team's big-play man.

So, for Pop Warner, the end had come. He had gained respect not only because of his ability to combine talent and deception to produce outstanding teams, but because he played clean football. "I don't believe anyone can play two kinds of football, good and dirty, at the same time," he once said. "I want my boys to play good football."

Of course, Pop had ways of bending the rules for "good" football.

"Glenn was never very active *on* the rules committee," Alonzo Stagg said. "But we'd make a rule and Glenn would think up a way to get around it . . . and we'd have to meet his challenge. He kept us on our toes, I can tell you."

Warner left for Stanford in 1924 and stayed until 1932, when he returned East to coach Temple, a move he said "was the worst mistake I ever made."

At Pitt, he was succeeded by one of his own pupils, former guard Jock Sutherland, who starred on Warner's 1915-16-17 teams. The master taught his pupil well. Jock Sutherland became Pitt's winningest head coach.

1924

Game 27

How Many Did He Miss?

The Teapot Dome scandal was making the Harding Administration look bad in Washington while Penn State was having an embarrassing time in State College trying to explain to its student body why it had dropped Navy from the schedule.

Pitt won its third game in a row over Penn State, 24-3, at Forbes Field. Actually, Pitt was already in the midst of making history in this series. The Panthers would win 14 in a row until 1939.

The talk following this game did not center so much on the Pitt heroes as it did on the game's goat, Panther kicker Milo Gwosden. He was without words in trying to explain how he missed four extra points and two field goals. It was the worst game in Gwosden's career.

Penn State took an early 3-0 lead on Jules Prevost's 36-yard field goal. Prevost got an assist on the three-pointer from Pitt center Marshall Johnson, whose bad snap resulted in a fumble, Penn State recovering.

Call it a gift because that's all the points Penn State got. Hugo Bezdek's boys never again threatened the Panther goal line. The Lions dragged their tails back home with the knowledge they had produced only three first downs. Pitt, on the other hand, chalked up 11.

Milo Gwosden, Pitt field goal kicker, 1924.

PITT'S GREAT FINISH CRUSHES PENN STATE

Panthers Tear Nittany Lion to Pieces After Bezdek's Crew Kick Field Goal in First Period; Pittsburgh Scores 24 Points

Fullback Andrew Gustafson scored Pitt's first touchdown in the second quarter from 11 yards out after Penn State's E. D. Lafferty let a punt trickle through his hands. B. V. McMillan recovered for Pitt.

Quarterback Jesse Brown gave Pitt a 12-3 lead in the third quarter on a touchdown run, then Gwosden, subbing for end John Kifer, tried to make up for his other miscues with a TD run that made it 18-3. Naturally, Gwosden blew his own extra point. Halfback D. McCutcheon accounted for Pitt's final score in the last quarter.

The season had been a dismal one for both Bezdek and Jock Sutherland. Penn State finished 6-3-1; Pitt was 5-3-1 under the Scotsman. "Stone Face" as his players called him (behind his back, of course) vowed things would improve. Three losses weren't tolerable under any circumstances. Sutherland kept his promise. The most games Pitt would lose in any one season for the remainder of his stay was two.

1925

Game 28

Panthers Get a New Lair

Pitt finally found a place it could call home in 1925. Up until 1909, the Panthers had played their home games at Exposition Park in Pittsburgh's North Side. From 1909–1924, "home" was Forbes Field.

The Panthers' new site, Pitt Stadium, had a seating capacity of 50,000 when it first opened. Later, 6,500 additional seats were added. Unlike Forbes Field, there were no steel beams to obstruct a spectator's sightline at Pitt Stadium. It was, and still is, one of finest facilities in which to watch a college football game.

The Pitt-Penn State debut in the new complex came on Nov. 26, 1925. Pitt continued its winning ways over Hugo Bezdek's Lions with a 23-7 victory on frozen turf, even though Penn State had a commanding statistical edge with 17 first downs to Pitt's 12.

Running backs Andrew Gustafson and Gibby Welch each scored for Pitt as did tackle A. J. Salata. Gustafson single-handedly beat Penn State by tallying 11 points, including a field goal and two extra points.

Just as they had done in the previous two years, the Lions scored first in the contest. And what they had done in the previous two years, the Lions scored first in the contest. And what a score it was! Talk about thrilling plays, this one was straight out of Bezdek's old gambling books. The chapter was probably titled, "When They

PANTHERS END GREAT SEASON

Beat Penn State for **Fourth** Straight Time — **Record-** Breaking Crowd **Sees Col-** orful Gridiron Battle

advantage of this break in their favor.

For Pitt, Capt. Chase sang his intercollegiate football swan song in tuneful voice. He was a power of the defense, many times not only putting his own opponent out of the play, but breaking through and grabbing the man with the ball far behind the letter's ____ ___

Least Expect It," because Jock Sutherland's team was caught totally off guard.

Penn State quarterback Cy Lungren directed the Lions to the Panther 25 on a series of passes. On fourth down, Pitt prepared for Penn State's field goal attempt as kicker Ken Weston entered the game. Lungren held for Weston, but when he received the snap, he threw to his wide-open halfback, Johnny Roepke, for a touchdown. Weston's PAT made it 7-0, Penn State.

Roepke's score was the Lions' first touchdown against Pitt since the 1919 game which Penn State won, 20-0.

Ahh, but he committed a cardinal sin later in the first quarter when a Bas Gray's pass eluded Roepke's grasp and Panther tackle A. J. Salata recovered the ball in midair, then raced 20 yards for a touchdown. Gustafson's point-after tied the game.

Gustafson finished the quarter by booting a 28-yard field goal that gave Pitt a 10-7 lead. Penn State had been offside on Gustafson's first try—which he missed—but the additional five yards were just enough to make good on the next attempt.

Pitt scored again in the last two quarters on Gustafson and Welch touchdowns. Welch's TD was an 80-yard sprint, then a series record.

Sutherland's squad ended the season 8-1-1. Tackle Ralph Chase was named to the All-American team. Chase was the first Panther to be so honored in four years. Penn State had its worst season (4-4-1) under Bezdek since the skipper's debut in 1918.

1926

Game 29

A Frightened Fawn

One reason why Pitt turned out so many dynamic teams at the start of the '20s was the abundance of talent in the Panther backfield. Two of the most prolific runners and scorers in Pitt football history were Tom Davies and Gilbert Welch, both of whom are members of Pitt's All-Time Team.

Gibby Welch saved some of his best moments on the gridiron for the annual Pitt-Penn State bash. In 1925, he rambled 80 yards for a touchdown, to break Karl Bohren's series record of 70 set two years earlier.

But on Nov. 25, 1926, Gibby Welch dazzled a standing room only crowd at Pitt Stadium (estimated 65,000) with two long touchdown runs as Pitt trampled Penn State, 24-6. Once again, the fleet-footed halfback from Parkersburg High had stolen the thunder from under Jock Sutherland's feet.

The *Philadelphia Inquirer* turned Perry Lewis loose for this one and he responded in typical fashion:

. . . it was a lion famished for victory, and its hungry eyes gleamed with lust for the kill as it crouched to spring upon the Panther that was to furnish a seasonal feast.

. . . the sleek gridiron beast that Jock Sutherland trained and unleashed on State today ripped and tore the Nittany Lion to shreds. And the sharpest talon in the devastating claws of the Panther was Gilbert Welsh (sic), halfback.

Gibby Welch, Pitt All-American, 1927.

Perry Lewis was never one to mince words when it came to describing the game he had just witnessed.

Following a scoreless first quarter, in which Pitt had withstood Penn State's challenge five yards from the goal line, Welsh gave Pitt a 7-0 lead with a 54-yard run. As Lewis wrote in his story, "Welch . . . darted through a hole at tackle and squirmed away from the secondary defense.

"Fleet tacklers pressed him over toward the sideline, and it seemed impossible for the runner to avoid stepping out of bounds on State's 34-yard line, but in some miraculous manner Welsh did keep within the playing field, at the same time tearing away from two tacklers to speed on down the field . . ."

Penn State came to within 7-6 that same quarter as halfback Johnny Roepke completed a 30-yard pass to Ken Weston, giving the Lions a first down on the Panther 4-yard line. Roepke crashed through tackle two downs later for the touchdown but missed his point-after kick.

Roepke's kicking misfortunes plagued him in the third quarter as well when he shanked a 23-yard field goal.

Pitt clung to its 7-6 lead as the fourth quarter began. Welch intercepted a Lion pass and ran it back 24 yards to the Penn State 45. Welch next caught an 18-yard pass from quarterback Fisher (first name unknown) to the State 27. Three plays later, James Rooney drop-kicked a 15-yard field goal, giving Pitt a 10-6 lead.

Rooney intercepted a Lion pass near midfield during the next series to set up Welch's final touchdown run. This one was only 35 yards but, in the words of Perry Lewis, Welch ran "like a frightened fawn around end." Welch's score made it 17-6.

Pitt's Joe Schmidt added another TD in the final minutes with a four-yard run. Oh yes, Welch helped set the stage for that score with an 18-yard run and eight-yard pass reception.

Considering the prominent role Gibby Welch played in this game, the game before and the game which would follow in 1927, it's difficult to understand how the *Inquirer* could botch his name in the headline. It probably had something to do with Lewis' having misspelled Welch's name in his story.

But in 1926, the *Inquirer* misspelled Welch's name at the top of its sports page in 24-point type.

Oh well, at least the Inky had the correct score.

1927

Game 30

Pop Comes Home

Pop Warner traveled all the way from Palo Alto, Calif., to see Jock Sutherland's Panthers smother Penn State, 30-0. Actually, Warner was anxious to see Gibby Welch, whom he had recruited just before leaving Pitt for Stanford.

Warner's special interest in this game had much to do with the fact that Pitt would probably meet Stanford in the Rose Bowl on New Year's Day.

Welch didn't disappoint his old friend as he treated Warner and 60,000 others at Pitt Stadium to several scintillating runs plus a touchdown. Welch, in fact, was on his way to All-America honors, although such distinction seemed a year overdue.

Welch not only provided yardage on the ground, he threw a couple of passes and handled the punting chores. By game's end, Pop Warner was said to have devised a defense to stop Welch's end runs should Pitt play Stanford.

Panther halfback Jimmy Hagan put Pitt on the board with a second-quarter safety, chasing Lion halfback John Miller behind the goal line before tackling him. Hagan next took Penn State's kick and dashed 22 yards to the Lion 33-yard line. Welch ripped off 26 more, then gave way to A. A. "Bullet" Booth, who ran it in from the seven, giving Pitt a 9-0 lead (Booth PAT).

Welch extended the lead to 16-0 in the third quarter, ripping into Penn State's line on seven occasions for 40 yards, before finally

Jock Sutherland, Pitt Head Coach, 1924 to 1938.

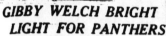

crossing the goal line. Booth then scored another touchdown in the final quarter after Penn State's Johnny Roepke fumbled the ball away at midfield.

Starting from the 50, Hagan ran for 20 yards, then Welch racked up 15 more to the Lion 15, setting things up for Booth's second score. Hagan tallied Pitt's last touchdown minutes later, making it 30-0.

Although Welch's runs had captivated everyone, Bullet Booth was the real story in this game with his two touchdowns and four PATs for 16 points.

Pitt compiled 22 first downs, Penn State five and finished the regular season at 8-0-1.

Pop Warner remarked, "That is the best team I have seen this season, and I have seen a lot of them. The backfield is well-nigh perfect, the line is powerful with tremendous charge, and Welch and Hagan are real stars."

Warner had taken accurate notes on this game. They proved to be beneficial several weeks later when Pitt traveled to the Rose Bowl in Pasadena for its first-ever post-season appearance. Not surprisingly, it was a defensive game as Stanford slipped past Pitt, 7-6.

Pop Warner, the old schoolmaster, had beaten his star pupil, Jock Sutherland.

1928

Game 31

Octavious Uansa

President Calvin Coolidge spent his Thanksgiving Day in Virginia watching North Carolina twice overcome Squire leads to win, 24-20.

Had the President elected to spend Nov. 29 in Western Pennsylvania, he would have seen a game that wasn't near as close in its competitiveness, but exciting, nonetheless. For it was at Pitt Stadium that one Octavious "Toby" Uansa ran back the opening kick 100 yards for a touchdown as Pitt routed Penn State, 26-0.

Uansa's feat is the longest runback in series history, and longest TD as well. In fact, only one Panther has ever returned a kick farther than Uansa. That would be—you guessed it—Gibby Welch, the man whose place Uansa took when Welch graduated. Welch ran back a kick 105 yards for a touchdown against West Virginia in 1927.

Uansa also scored on a 44-yard run and his play at safety earned him the Most Valuable Player Award in the 1928 contest.

Penn State seemed stunned by Uansa's early score and its receivers spent the better part of the afternoon dropping passes that should have been caught. The Lions secured only three first downs, all via forward passes. Penn State's only true scoring opportunity came late in the game after Uansa fumbled deep inside Panther territory.

He atoned for that sin, however, by intercepting Coop French's pass, and then ran the ball out of harms way.

Jock Sutherland again frustrated Lion Coach Hugo Bezdek by

Pitt Varsity team, 1929.

cutting off Penn State's outside threats, forcing the Lions to run inside against the Panthers' huge linemen.

One irony in this game concerns Pitt's outstanding tackle, Mike Getto, who was injured early in the game and never returned to the lineup. Pitt seemed to play even harder without Getto. His absence was never felt in the game. Getto, by the way, was Pitt's only All-American in 1928.

Sutherland's team ended its season that afternoon with a 6-2-1 record. Bezdek, meanwhile, concluded his worst year on Mt. Nittany with a 3-5-1 record. In retrospect, Bezdek's best years were behind him now. He would coach one more season before leaving football altogether to become Penn State's athletic director. Actually, the move to fire Bezdek had begun some time earlier in of all places, Pittsburgh, where a strong and influential pocket of PSU alums were plotting his ouster.

1929

Game 32

Make Room for Parkinson

As the series progressed fans were being treated yearly to one-man performances. All the while, it was Pitt that was doing the performing starting with Andrew Gustafson, then Gibby Welch, Bullet Booth, and Toby Uansa.

With so many outstanding players in front of him, it was a wonder Tom Parkinson ever got his chance in this series, his moment in the sun, so to speak.

In 1929 the Pitt fullback finally surfaced as a major force in the rivalry. Parkinson rushed for 182 yards, a record then, and scored all 20 points as the Panthers devoured Penn State, 20-7, for their eighth straight conquest. Parkinson scored three touchdowns and added two PATs.

For the eighth straight year Hugo Bezdek watched silently as one Pitt player outscored his entire team.

As in the recent past, Penn State led in this one only to see the game slip away. The Lions held a slim 7-6 lead in the third quarter when Parkinson scored his second touchdown to decide the game.

Pitt launched an 85-yard, 16-play drive with Parkinson carrying the ball 11 times for a 13-7 lead. Bezdek had instructed his defense to concentrate on stopping Uansa in this game. The Lions handled that chore very well, but while they were keying on Uansa, Parkinson was doing all the damage.

Penn State coaches, Dutch Hermann, Dick Harlow and Hugo Bezdek.

Parkinson scored from short yardage midway into the first quarter to give Pitt a 6-0 lead. The 60-yard drive was highlighted by several unusual triple passes and fake reverses around the ends with Parkinson and halfback William Walinshus. The latter had the longest run in the drive, that being 15 yards. Parkinson missed his own point-after, but he was perfect the remainder of the afternoon at Pitt Stadium.

Penn State scored its only touchdown in the second quarter on a 23-yard pass from quarterback Coop French to his end, Skip Stahley. Yutz Diedrich's extra point gave the Lions their only lead in the game, 7-6.

Pitt then launched the 85-yard drive that culminated with Parkinson's second touchdown, which put the Panthers in front to stay.

Pitt's final touchdown drive began on the Panther 16-yard line late in the fourth quarter. Parkinson ripped through the State line for 18 yards to the 34. Uansa added his efforts to give Pitt another first down across midfield. The rest of the drive saw Uansa and Parkinson alternate handoffs before the latter finally plunged into the end zone from the two. Parkinson's PAT made the final 20-7.

The victory was the beginning of better things for the Panthers. Even though Pitt got crushed by Southern Cal, 47-14, in the Rose Bowl, Jock Sutherland's team was voted National Champion along with Notre Dame.

Pitt's 9-1 record was the best since Pop Warner's 1917 squad went 9-0. Oddly enough, that team, which Sutherland starred on as an All-American center, was not voted best in the country.

Sutherland's 1929 squad was, despite an awful loss. Four Panthers captured All-American honors—Uansa, Parkinson, guard Ray Montgomery and end Joe Donchess.

As for Hugo Bezdek, the 6-3 season—his last—had been a disappointing one. His 12-year record at Penn State was 65-30-11. Bob Higgins replaced him. Bezdek died a lonely man in Atlantic City in 1952.

1930

Game 33

Who's Our Quarterback?

The *Philadelphia Inquirer* headline tooted the good and bad news for local readers: "UPPER DARBY HIGH LAD WINS FOR PANTHERS," it said.

Warren Heller was a standout high school performer in the Philadelphia suburbs. Now he was a sophomore halfback for Jock Sutherland's Panthers. Heller broke Tom Parkinson's 1929 record of 182 yards rushing with his 200-yard, two touchdown performance as Pitt outlasted Penn State, 19-12. Heller scored on runs of 31 and 80 yards.

The Thanksgiving Day crowd at Pitt Stadium numbered barely 20,000. They braved sub-zero temperatures to see Pitt finish up a 6-2-1 season.

Heller's scores were part of a trilogy. On both touchdowns, he darted through right tackle, turned on the afterburners, and outran Penn State's two best defenders, Coop French, who doubled as quarterback, and Yutz Diedrich.

The intense cold hindered both teams. Neither seemed able to do anything with the football in the opening quarter. Pitt's first near touchdown was the result of a short Penn State punt, but that was because the ball was virtually frozen.

The Panthers' began attacking from their own 36-yard line. Heller and fullback Franklin Hood drove the ball all the way to the Lions' 2-yard line but couldn't put it over in four cracks.

Pitt's defense was equally belligerent. State could move no farther than the 5 and was forced to punt from behind the goal line. Paul Reider fielded the ball and returned it to the Penn State 36.

Heller ran a reverse for five yards, then dashed 31 more on second down for his first score. Pitt led 6-0.

Penn State tied the game, 6-6, at early in the third quarter on George Lasich's one-yard dive. The big play for the Lions was French's 38-yard pass to Diedrich, who reached the Pitt 2-yard line before Heller knocked him out of bounds. Two tries up the middle paved the way for Lasich's score. Diedrich attempted to pass for the extra point, but the ball smacked into the ground.

The ball exchanged hands one more time before Pitt scored its second touchdown.

Following Diedrich's missed 25-yard field goal, Pitt took over on its 20. On first down, Heller burst through tackle and rambled 80 yards for the score. Ed Baker's kick gave Pitt a 13-6 lead heading into the last quarter.

A little bit of a gamble paid off in dividends as Pitt scored its third touchdown. Pitt marched 70 yards but the final 32 were the important ones. Penn State was expecting Pitt to run on first from the 32 and adjusted its defense accordingly. After all, Pitt had been running the ball all afternoon and with much success. Why pass now?

But that's just what Jock Sutherland ordered his team to do. Jock wanted one more insurance touchdown. The word went to Pitt captain Ed Baker.

Heller fired a pass to Paul Reider, who made a pretty catch at the 8-yard line before being tackled on the 4. Pitt failed to cross the goal line, however, on the next three tries. Hmm? More strategy was going on in Sutherland's mind.

Baker was *technically* the quarterback. When Pitt lined up for fourth down, though, Hood, the fullback, was standing over center and Baker along the line of scrimmage. Hood threw the final two yards to Baker and it was 19-6, following his own PAT.

Sutherland made liberal substitutions, then sweated out the final minutes as Penn State immediately blocked a Panther punt and turned it into a touchdown. Earle Edwards got his hand on Harry Wagner's punt at the Pitt 40, then recovered the ball and danced into the endzone untouched. It was now 19-12.

Lion Coach Bob Higgins ordered French to throw the ball in the waning minutes as Penn State desperately tried to tie it up, but time

Beaver Field, Penn State's first home.

ran out.

Worldwide economic depression had set in following the stock market crash in 1929. But in State College, Pa., Penn State fans had been feeling a different kind of depression for over a decade. You see, it had been 12 years since Penn State last defeated Pitt. The wait would get longer.

1931

Game 34

Home Not So Sweet Home

Twenty-nine years has passed since Penn State last played a home game (1902) at Beaver Field. By now, the stadium had been enlarged to accommodate 30,000 spectators. Lion Coach Bob Higgins was hoping its friendly confines would be an ally in the 1931 game. Lord knows, Penn State needed some additional help, having lost nine in a row.

Friendly confines, they were not. Pitt stormed ahead with four first-quarter touchdowns to maul Penn State 41-6, the worst defeat the Lions have ever suffered in this series, although their 48-14 loss in 1981 figures to be remembered for some time to come.

The all-time lopsided loss was the 59-0 beating Pitt suffered in 1903.

Penn State was hexed from the start with a bad case of fumblitis. The first one came just two minutes into the game and gave Pitt an early 6-0 lead. Lion halfback Phil Moonves was the guilty party.

Moonves dropped the opening kickoff, giving Pitt the ball on the Penn State 16-yard line. Pitt's Mr. Simms smashed into the line four times before going over.

State received the next kickoff and started out on its 20. Again the ball went to Moonves, who fumbled it away after a four-yard gain. On Pitt's first play, Simms slashed 24 yards for a touchdown. Rocco

Cutri's extra point put Pitt ahead 13-0. Cutri booted five PATs in this game, missing the uprights just once.

There were still 12 minutes left to play in the opening quarter, just enough time for Pitt to add two more touchdowns, making it 27-0. The 10,000 who braved the cold weather might have been better off going home because this one was over before it began.

Pitt scored twice more in the second and third quarters, the Panthers' last score being the highlight of the day when Dick Matesic intercepted a Don Conn pass, then scooted 60 yards for the score. It was Matesic's second TD of the game.

Conn helped the Lions to their only score in the third quarter with a short pass to Bill McMillan. Pitt was unsatisfied with having yielded those six points, and added injury to insult by blocking the extra point.

Higgins made wholesale substitutions in an effort to revive the Lions' lifeless attack but it was in vain. Panther Coach Jock Sutherland, who still had not lost to a Penn State team either as a player or coach, threw in his third and fourth string in the second half. By the third quarter's end, the only regular in the lineup was running back Jim Clark, who scored the touchdown that made it 34-0.

Cutri, incidentally, was not only the kicker in this game but also the quarterback. Sutherland ordered him not to run or throw the ball in the second half, just block.

Overall, Pitt tried just six passes, completing one. The lone reception was by Panther end Joe Skladany, a future All-American. Skladany took a Matesic pass 20 yards to set up the latter's second quarter TD.

Conn completed six of 12 passes, including his scoring pass to McMillan.

Newspaper accounts from the Oct. 31 game said that Penn State was thoroughly demoralized after the first quarter and played in such a manner till the finish.

The game departed from tradition in that it was played midway into the season.

And what a terrible season it was for Penn State. The Lions finished 2-8, their only victories coming against Lebanon Valley and Lehigh. Penn State was just beginning its "down period" in football history. Higgins would only win 15 games over the next five years.

Sutherland's Panthers finished 8-1 and were voted National Champions in the Davis poll while Southern Cal was the favorite in both the AP and UPI wire polls. It was Sutherland's second national title and Pitt's fifth overall.

Panthers Defeat Penn State

Nittany Lion Easy Victim In Grid Tilt

Sutherland Eleven Piles Up 27 Points During First Quarter

STATE SCORES ONCE

Local Reserves Bear Brunt in Flashing Aerial, Line-Plunge Game

STATE COLLEGE, Pa., Oct. .. —Without using a first team man the Golden Panthers of Pittsburgh defeated Penn State for the tenth straight year today before an alumni home-coming crowd of 10 thousand. The score was 41 to 6, and the Panthers had a lead

The started off with a rush, a touchdown before the was two minutes old and addit econd within less than a minut later. From then on until

Schwartz Makes 12 Yards Fo

Oregon Beats N.Y.U., 14-6

Kansas Eleven Be West Virginia,

The Pitt-Penn State series took a holiday from 1932-1934. The series now saw Pitt ahead in victories, 19-13-2. Pitt led in scoring, too, 417-336. Think about that for a moment. Through the first 25 games, the Panthers had amassed only 190 points; yet in the last nine meetings following 1922, they had outscored Penn State, 227-44!

1935

Game 35

"Grotesque Football"

The series resumed for the 35th meeting at Pitt Stadium on Oct. 26, 1935. The result was the same (Pitt won) as it was when Pitt and Penn State last met in 1931. Only the place had changed. The *Pittsburgh Press* was uncharacteristically tough on Pitt after the Panthers fought to a 9-0 victory before a mostly empty stadium (18,000).

The *Press* said Pitt had played "grotesque" football and accused Jock Sutherland's team, which was the reigning National Champion of 1934, of appearing "infrequently robust." On the other hand, the story by Chester L. Smith, *Press* sports editor, hailed Penn State's defense as "brilliant."

Pitt had as many as 10 opportunities to score and save for a field goal by Frank Patrick and his late touchdown, Penn State's defense would not yield when pressured. Much of the credit there went to Lion guard Jack Economos. The sophomore from (Pittsburgh) Schenley High was virtually indestructible on the line, making several touchdown-saving tackles. Economos was greeted with a well-deserved standing ovation when Lion Coach Bob Higgins pulled him at the end of the game.

Another Lion who deserved recognition, though he didn't get a standing "O," was left tackle Bob Weber. Penn State's captain had played the entire 60 minutes that crisp, autumn afternoon.

Patrick, the latest in a long line of Panther fullbacks, kicked his

Lions Stage
Great Fight
But Weaken

Patrick Scores Field Goal
And Touchdown For
All Panther Points

ONLY 18,000 LOOK ON

Sutherland Scythe Commits
Many Errors, Meets
Stubborn Defense

Lion Silenced

game-winning 11-yard field goal with 59 seconds remaining in the third quarter. Pitt seemed to breathe a sigh of relief after that and his touchdown early in the fourth quarter bolstered the Panthers' sagging spirits.

"Sutherland Scythe," as the *Press* referred to Pitt's club, could not understand how a team could be so stubborn. Pitt gained 329 yards in this game, yet had only one touchdown to show for it. Penn State managed a meager 72 yards. Pitt had 11 first downs while Penn State had four. But Pitt had also turned the ball over three times on fumbles.

Penn State never crossed Pitt's 28-yard line and failed to escape its own end of the field in the second half. Still, Higgins' squad wouldn't roll over and play dead. Instead, they harassed Pitt's ballcarriers — Leo Malarkey, Leon Shedlosky and Patrick — and batted down quarterback Arnold Greene's passes.

Three times Penn State's defense, its back to the wall, met the challenge and prevented Pitt from scoring inside the 5-yard line. Most who watched it then would probably tell you it was the best defensive duel since the 1930 game which Pitt won, 19-12.

The best individual rushing effort was Shedlosky's 48-yard run in the first quarter. Shedlosky appeared to have an easy touchdown until Economos tackled him near the Lion 40-yard line. Pitt drove deeper into Lion territory before its drive died on the Lion 4-yard line.

Sutherland's boys had a bit of an off-year with a 7-1-2 record. They lost 9-6 to Notre Dame and suffered through 0-0 ties with Fordham and Carnegie Tech.

Penn State lost to Bucknell on a safety (2-0) to finish its season with a dismal 4-4 record. Things were fairly awful on Mt. Nittany, where Penn State hadn't finished above .500 since 1929 (6-3).

As Higgins later realized, the stock market wasn't the only thing that crashed. But the economy recovered a little sooner than the Lions' football program.

1936

Game 36

Diced by the Scythe

Nicknames. The Pitt-Penn State series is loaded with them . . . Irish McIlveen, Bull McCleary, Hoot Flanagan, Bullet Booth, and so on.

The 1936 clash saw several nicknamed players colliding with each other. On the Pitt side you had "Mad Marshall" Goldberg and "Curly" Harold Stebbins. On the Penn State side there was "Windy" Wear. What a collection of characters.

Pitt's cast was the stronger of the two as the final score would indicate: 34-7. Though the end result would belie such, this game was much closer than that. Penn State trailed 14-7 heading into the fourth quarter.

What is somewhat puzzling about this game is why Pitt Coach Jock Sutherland went with a makeshift unit of second-string players in the third frame, thereby allowing Penn State to come back. Hell, Sutherland could have lost the game. It didn't make sense.

Nor did the fact there were 10 fumbles on a dry field. Penn State inexplicably coughed up the football six times, losing four of them. Pitt fumbled four times but twice recovered.

Reporters covering the game mocked Penn State's "comeback" given these circumstances and mused that Sutherland was toying with the Nittany Lions to please the 19,000 who showed up at Pitt Stadium that afternoon.

As the *Pittsburgh Press* wise-cracked, ". . . they (Lions) chose to

"Mad Marshall" Goldberg, Pitt All-American, 1937 and 1938. He scored three touchdowns in the 1936 game.

make the most of their opportunity, more power to them."

The Lions' abortive comeback began when State's sprite backs, Wear and Harrison, moved Penn State from its own 35 across midfield to the Pitt 46-yard line. Wear zipped through the line for 35 yards to the 11 for a first down. Then, Lion Coach Bob Higgins pulled a cute little prank that today would probably get you a penalty.

Higgins instructed Harrison to stand over on the far sideline, just in bounds. In other words, give the appearance he was on the sideline, not in the play.

After hurrying to line up, Penn State called a quick count as Wear, who was not the starting quarterback in this game, let fly down the sideline to Harrison. The Lion halfback was wide open simply because none of the Panther defenders had seen him in the play. Harrison's easy score and Joe Metro's kick cut Pitt's lead to 14-7.

While State's players were congratulating themselves for this tricky bit of playcalling, Pitt was seething with anger. Jock Sutherland's boys weren't to be fooled with, especially in this, the year they would recapture the National Championship.

Penn State rested on its laurels for a brief moment. What followed were four Panther touchdowns that wiped the smiles off everyone dressed in Blue & White.

The duo of Marshall Goldberg and Harold Stebbins were to provide the first ripple in Pitt's tidal wave. Earlier Goldberg had flipped a 25-yard scoring pass to Stebbins giving Pitt a 7-0 lead. Then in the third quarter Goldberg directed an 80-yard drive which culminated with Frank Patrick's touchdown making it 14-0. Mad Marshall had carried the ball 10 times for 65 yards.

Now it was the last quarter and Penn State was making a game of it. Goldberg and Stebbins mapped out their strategy. Stebbins went 39 yards off an end run to the Lion 32. Goldberg then reeled off the opposite flank for 15 more to the Penn State 17. Stebbins slammed into the line a few more times before finally scoring from four yards out. 20-7.

Halfback Johnny Wood, one of Sutherland's bench warmers that game, added a touchdown moments later. 27-7. The wave was starting to curl. Higgins' club was stunned. In less than 8 minutes, the game had swung the other way.

Lion halfback John Patrick fumbled near midfield right into the arms of Panther defensive back Johnny Urban. Urban made a quick cut around one man, then lurched downfield for a 44-yard TD. 34-7. The wave had leveled everything in its path.

Jock Sutherland, Pitt Head Coach , never lost to Penn State as a player and coach.

Pitt went on to defeat Nebraska and Carnegie Tech before heading for the Rose Bowl, where it clinched the National Championship with a resounding 21-0 victory over Washington.

The Sutherland Scythe finished 8-1-1 while presenting its mentor with his fourth national title in eight years. One more still awaited him.

1937

Game 37

The Pollsters

The wire service polls awarded the National Championship to Minnesota in 1936 while both the Illustrated Football Annual (IFA) and The Football Thesaurus (TFT) gave Pitt the nod.

Because there were so many rating systems—12 to be exact—there was really never such a thing as an undisputed champion, save for those rare moments when everyone agreed. For instance, in 1916 and 1918, Pittsburgh was a unanimous choice among the cantankerous bodies which insisted that their's and their's alone was the true yardstick by which champions were to be measured.

By 1970, only AP and UPI remained to honor America's collegiate heroes. The former being the writer/broadcaster poll and the latter, the NCAA coaches poll. If you want to narrow the field down to an imprecise science, which any rating system is, AP is the generally accepted poll by which a champion is determined.

Nevertheless, most schools recognize any championships awarded during the era of numerous pollsters. That's why it may surprise you that Pitt lists ALL nine of its titles even though only three were by unanimous consent.

So, Jock Sutherland's Panthers were the 1936 champs, by their own count, and 1937 was to be no different. In fact, six pollsters said so at the conclusion of the season even though Pitt wasn't even invited to a bowl!

Penn State was still mired in mediocrity with a 5-2 record when it travelled to Pitt Stadium on Nov. 20, to meet No. 1 ranked Pitt. The weather was cold and the field blanketed in white—the kind of snowy atmosphere Penn State was accustomed to in Central Pennsylvania.

No matter. Pitt still won the game, 28-7. Mad Marshall Goldberg tallied three touchdowns as Pitt ripped open a 21-0 gap in the first half that sealed the Lions' fate.

Goldberg, who would later play as a professional with the Chicago Cardinals and join the Panther Hall of Fame (1958), was about to become an All-American along with guard/kicker Frank Souchak, center Bill Daddio, and end Tony Matisi.

Patrick gave Pitt a 7-0 lead in the first quarter, completing a 55-yard drive sparked by two Goldberg runs of 14 and 12 yards. Okay, they weren't long gainers, but every little chunk of real estate eventually adds up to a piece of property.

Goldberg paced a second drive that quarter of 46 yards, scoring on a one-yard run to make it 14-0. His second touchdown in the next quarter decided matters at 21-0.

Penn State gained some satisfaction with Spike Alter's 30-yard scoring pass from Steve Rollins. Those were the only points the Lions could roar about.

Goldberg collected his third touchdown in the fourth period with a seven-yard run. The madman did most of the work during the 54-yard drive, too. By then, Sutherland had thrown his reserves into the game. But not before all 19 of his seniors had played at least one down.

Pitt shut out Duke 10-0, to close out the season with a 9-0-1 record. Dr. John Bain Sutherland had won his fifth national title, unprecedented in school history. Now the only worlds left to conquer were a few more victories.

1938

Game 38

End of an Era

The Dream Backfield, that's what people in Pittsburgh were calling Jock Sutherland's running game. Dick Cassiano at left halfback, Curly Harold Stebbins at right halfback and Mad Marshall Goldberg, playing a new position, fullback. Johnny Chickerneo was the quarterback.

Pitt had back-to-back national titles and Mad Marshall, despite his lack of weight (185 pounds) had agreed to Sutherland's wish that he become a fullback. So versatile was Goldberg, he was able to become a well-respected blocker in just a season.

What had gone almost unnoticed, also because of Goldberg's outstanding offensive talents, was his play at defensive back. For three years, the product of Elkins, West Virginia, had played solidly on defense while everyone around him hailed his offensive performances. But when Goldberg joined the pro football Cardinals, it was as a defensive back, not halfback.

Pitt rolled over Penn State, 26-0, at Pitt Stadium on Nov. 19. It was Sutherland's farewell game in Pittsburgh. Goldberg played sparingly because of a leg injury. It too, was his last home game. Only 14,000 were on hand to see it because of a drizzling rain that turned the field into a mud bowl.

And although one-third of the Dream Backfield spent most of the day on the bench, another third rained on Penn State.

Cassiano scored three touchdowns to overshadow the many

seniors around him who no doubt planned to capture the spotlight during Senior Day. To make matters worse, a sophomore, Bob Thurbon, had scored the Panthers' other touchdown. Rudeness!

The chilly wetness made the ball difficult to carry and impossible to throw. Pitt led 7-0 at the half on Cassiano's touchdown run of 16 yards. Lloyd Ickes helped Pitt's cause by fumbling the ball away at the Penn State 46-yard line. On the turnover, Cassiano clicked off runs of 25 and 16 yards, the last being his TD run.

After sitting out the second quarter, Goldberg started the second half in a blaze of glory with a 53-yard kickoff run to Penn State's 44, where Ickes, the last man between Mad Marshall and the goalposts, brought him down.

Goldberg next ran the ball to the 19 before yielding to Cassiano, who scored off a reverse end run to make it 13-0. Cassiano's final score, a 28-yard dash around end, came moments later. Pitt had a 21-0 cushion.

By then, the Panthers were thinking only of their final game of the season at Duke, which was unbeaten and untied.

Duke won, however, 7-0. Pitt finished 8-2, ranked eighth by AP. Daddio and Goldberg made the All-American squad and TCU was voted National Champion.

The Sutherland era of Pitt had ended after 15 years, 111 victories, 20 losses and 12 ties. Plus five national championships. Is it any wonder why most Pittsburghers consider Jock Sutherland the school's greatest coach?

After a coaching stint at Brooklyn, Sutherland entered the Navy in 1941. Upon his return, Jock coached the Pittsburgh Steelers to glory until his unexpected death in 1948.

Sutherland's biggest accomplishment, one which people often forget, is in his 15 years as the Panthers' coach and four years as a star player, Pitt never lost to Penn State.

Two things, however, mar his memory. Former Panther Jimmy Hagan as athletic director, decided to deemphasize Pitt's schedule that season. How ironic considering Notre Dame had deemphasized its years earlier by dropping Pitt after suffering losses to Sutherland. Sutherland would not stand for patsy opponents. So he quit, saying, "The future athletic course is so indefinite and vague that . . . it will be for the best interests of all concerned if I ask you to accept my resignation."

The second was not Jock's own doing. On April 7, 1948, after a series of excruciating headaches, a tumor in Sutherland's brain ruptured. He had been in Kentucky scouting when it happened. A milkman in Bandana found the Scotsman walking aimlessly through the town.

Perhaps the most poignant memory of this great man is that of John Michelosen, his quarterback in 1937, leaving Kentucky with the near lifeless body of Jock Sutherland. Four days and two operations later, Sutherland died.

Grantland Rice wrote:

There's a fog now over Scotland, and a mist on
Pittsburgh's field;
No valiant hand to flash the sword or hold the
guiding shield.
There's a big, braw fellow missing from the golden land
of fame.
For Jock Sutherland has left us—and the game is not
the same.

1939

Game 39

Lions Finally Win One

Charles Bowser took the reins from Jock Sutherland. Imagine how difficult it was to replace a living legend. To make his task even harder, Bowser did something unthinkable, something that the mighty Sutherland had never done—he lost a game to Penn State. Worse yet, a shutout!

The score was 10-0. For the famished Lions, it was the first series victory in 20 years. Coincidentally, it came during a season when Penn State (5-1-2) would finish with a better record than Pitt (5-4).

Only 20,000 people were on hand at Beaver Field to share this magic moment, but that was enough to help Lion Coach Bob Higgins forget about the past six games played in this series. Games in which his club scored a mere 32 points en route to losing each. So ecstatic were the people in State College with this thrilling victory that the University administration declared the following Monday a holiday. Yep, no classes.

Fullback Bill Smaltz scored the game's only touchdown in the first quarter and placekicker John Patrick, who had booted a winning field goal over Penn two weeks earlier, ensured the win with a fourth-quarter field goal.

Until the closing minutes of the game, Pitt never ventured beyond Penn State's 30-yard line. Also, it was the first—and only—time that season the Panthers were held scoreless.

Penn State gained 240 yards and accumulated 17 first downs,

more than any amount in the past decade, while holding Pitt to just nine and 165 yards on the ground.

Patrick attempted a 20-yard field goal late in the first quarter but his boot went wide. Pitt took over from there but on the Panthers' first play, senior halfback Dick Cassiano fumbled and Penn State's Leon Gajecki recovered at the Pitt 22.

Halfback Chuck Peters went off-tackle for three yards. His back-field partner, Craig White, took a reverse around left end for 18 more to the Pitt 1-yard line, setting up Smaltz' score. Ben Pollock's extra point made it 7-0. Pollock, by the way, set a personal record with that PAT. It was his 18th successful kick in 21 attempts. Not bad back then, but pretty insignificant in light of Herb Menhardt's school-record 54-for-54 set between 1979-80.

Peters and reserve back Lloyd Ickes drove the Lions 37 yards in the final quarter to the Panther 17 before Patrick booted his field goal, making it 10-0.

Pitt attempted a rally at the end, but Penn State wouldn't let this one slip away.

Even though the Lions weren't going to a bowl, several groups of fans rushed onto the field afterward to carry their heroes off. Bob Higgins was a winner—finally.

Pitt meanwhile, would suffer through some bad times in the seasons that followed. During the war years (1939-42) the school discontinued scholarships, as well as the practice of selecting team captains. The quality of players coming to Pitt in the next few years would not bring about any championships. Many other schools around the country were facing a similar crisis.

The greatest conflict, however—World War II—was being fought in Europe.

1940

Game 40

What About that Harmon Fellow?

Looking back now, this game, played on Nov. 23, pales in comparison to The Big One that was underway at Ohio Stadium that same afternoon.

While Pitt fullback George Kracum was going about his work scoring two touchdowns and setting up another during Pitt's 20-7 upset of Penn State, some 300 miles west of Pittsburgh, Tom Harmon was scoring three touchdowns, throwing passes for two more, kicking four conversions, rushing for 139 yards . . . and playing 59 minutes in Michigan's 40-0 pummeling of Ohio State.

George Kracum may have delighted 31,000 at Pitt Stadium, but what Harmon did before nearly 74,000 in Columbus ranks up there as one of the greatest, if not *THE* greatest, single-game performances in college football history. Indeed, Harmon was the big story of the day, unless you read the *Philadelphia Inquirer,* which casually mentioned it on its lead sports page the next morning.

Now that you know about Harmon's feats, we can proceed with Kracum's accomplishments in Pittsburgh.

Penn State came into the game seeking a bowl bid. All the Lions got from this one, however, was their first defeat against six wins and a tie. Penn State, led by center Leon Gajecki, a member of the famed "Seven Mountains," brought an ample supply of confidence

George Kracum, Pitt halfback, scored two touchdowns in the 1940 game.

into the game. Only West Virginia and Syracuse had been able to move the ball and score on the Lions' blocks of granite.

But then came Kracum. Along with teammate Ralph Fife, they put the Panthers in the lead in the first quarter running right at Penn State's huge linemen. Kracum raced 44 yards around end to the Penn State 5, then lateralled to Fife as he was being tackled. That clever maneuver paid off as Fife crossed the goal line for a 6-0 lead.

The score stayed that way until the third quarter when Edgar Jones, Pitt's left halfback, tossed a nifty 20-yard scoring pass to Bobby Thurbon, making it 13-0.

State had to play catch-up in the last quarter as the seconds ticked away. The Lions' only scoring drive began after Bill Smaltz intercepted a pass at his 30 and returned it to the Panther 47. A series of passes advanced the ball to the Pitt 14. On first down, Smaltz pitched to John Patrick, who danced into the end zone, cutting Penn State's deficit to 13-7.

Lion Coach Bob Higgins instructed Smaltz and Patrick to throw when Penn State got the ball back. That's exactly what they did. One of Patrick's passes got away from him and big George Kracum was there to make sure it found a comfortable home in his arms. Kracum intercepted the ball on the Lion 35 and scored the clinching touchdown that squeezed the last remaining breath from the Lions' lungs.

Pitt had avenged its loss of a year ago and dashed Penn State's bowl hopes in the process. It was something the Blue and Gold could take comfort in after a 3-4-1 season.

1941

Game 41

Special Delivery; Wrong Address

Penn State's winless famine of the '20s and '30s was still a sore point for Nittany Lion fans even as the '40s moved on. No Penn State team had beaten Pitt on its home soil since 1919. And none had scored more than 20 points since 1912.

Both bugaboos came to a screeching halt Nov. 22, 1941 as Penn State, clawing its way to a 7-2 season, stomped Pitt, 31-7, before 33,000 at Pitt Stadium.

If it's true the postman always rings twice, then it can be safely said that the Panthers' Edgar "Special Delivery" Jones missed a calling as he scored only once in the game.

The Pitt senior, who by now had accumulated a variety of nicknames based on the U.S. Postal System, was outdone on the field by Penn State's Johnny "Pepper" Petrella. He scored three touchdowns. The Lions' other Italian Stallion, Ralph Ventresco, added the last TD in the fourth quarter.

Although Petrella did not start at halfback, he delivered two touchdowns entering the lineup during the second quarter.

Defensively, Penn State employed a diamond defense to contain Jones' outside running threats while conceding passes. Except Jones completed only one of seven passes he threw. Pitt's only touchdown came on a Penn State mistake.

A study in contrasting moods from the 1941 game. Top photo shows Penn State coach Bob Higgins with players, and bottom photo shows dejected Pitt players.

Halfback Bill Debler fumbled a punt on his 48 in the opening quarter. Although Pitt was forced to punt, the next exchange found the Panthers on the Lions' 40-yard line. Jones scored from that distance on a weak-side reverse, but got an able block from Frank Saksa at the 10 which freed him the remainder of the way. Pitt led 7-0.

Pitt eventually got the back ball back, but Penn State backed the Panthers to the goal line where Jones' fourth-down punt traveled an amazing 56 yards. Lion fullback Bill Smaltz zipped a 30-yard completion to Aldo Cenci, easily the highlight of the drive, before Petrella took over. State drove to the Pitt 13 and on four tries, the little halfback finally scored to tie it up at 7-7.

Pitt fumbled the ball away on the ensuing kickoff, clearing the way for Penn State's second touchdown. Starting from the Panther 13, Petrella went five yards on a sweep, then four to the opposite side. Smaltz gained two more for the first down, then yielded to Petrella who scored, giving Penn State a 14-7 edge.

Though Pitt received the second-half kickoff, it could muster no offense and Jones was again obliged to punt. Penn State wasted little time in marching 51 yards to take an imposing 21-7 lead. Several nine-and 10-yard gains by Smaltz, Krouse and Petrella methodically moved the Lions to the Pitt 24, from where Petrella rambled into the end zone, smashing one Pitt defender along the way with a stiff forearm shiver.

Jones fumbled later in the quarter at his 16; Penn State recovered and Smaltz booted a field goal to make it 24-7. Smaltz also kicked all four Lion PATs in this contest.

Pitt continued to have trouble holding onto the football for any sustained period of time. Ventresco ripped two long gainers that moved the ball from the Pitt 45 to the 25. A Smaltz pass got it to the 5 before Ventresco scored Penn State's last touchdown.

Some say this was the most decisive victory in the first 41 years of the rivalry. That's subject to debate. All that is certain is Pitt crossed midfield just once in this game and garnered only four first downs amid 215 total yards.

Penn State churned out 14 first downs and 375 yards offense. Decisive, yes. But probably not the most decisive victory in the series. Don't forget, there was that 59-0 Lion fiasco back in 1903.

Still, Penn State's 1941 win was special. It ruined a dinner party given in the honor of Special Delivery Jones, who had played his final game in a Pitt jersey. Tommy Davies, a freshman All-American under Pop Warner in 1918 was the toastmaster.

1942

Game 42

Run for Daylight

The week before meeting Pittsburgh, Larry Joe provided some thrilling moments in Philadelphia where he paced Penn State's 13-7 victory over Penn at Franklin Field. Joe was a splendid runner who did nothing to disappoint the crowds waiting to see a quick burst of yardage.

Joe had already shown Penn his fancy footsteps, and now it was time to entertain Pitt. Joe broke a scoreless duel in the third quarter with a 90-yard kickoff return as the Lions nipped Pitt, 14-6, before a mere 12,000 at Beaver Field. In case you're counting, the victory marked the first time since 1911-12 that Penn State had won two games in a row from Pitt.

Joe's kickoff TD is the fourth best in series history. The all-time record is shared by Pitt's Toby Uansa (1928) and Penn State's Curt Warner (1979), both of whom ran back kicks 100 yards for scores.

Philadelphia Inquirer reporter Frank O'Gara captured Joe's historic feat with these words: "Shattering a 30-minute deadlock of desultory action with an exploit of 16 sparkling seconds, Joe grabbed the second-half kickoff and sped 90 yards for a touchdown that won the game."

Actually, it was Wilbur Van Lenten who won the game with his extra-point, because Pitt scored later that quarter, but missed the PAT.

Joe's runback was aided in large part by a brutal downfield block from Penn State's massive quarterback, of all people, Aldo Cenci.

Larry Joe, Penn State halfback, on a 90-yard kickoff–return TD, 1942.

Unlike many game-breaking runs you see today, Larry Joe's involved no fancy footwork, no dodging of opponents, just simple straight-down-the-field running from the time he took Walt West's kick at the 10, till he crossed the goal line.

It was almost as if someone had cleared a lane down the center of the field for Joe to run through. A desperate attempted tackle by Pitt end Mike Stocak failed near the goal line.

Pitt came back with six points on West's touchdown at the quarter's end to make it 7-6, but Cenci gave the Lions an insurance touchdown off a 48-yard drive accounting for the 14-6 final.

Larry Joe entered the service shortly after the season and did not return to Penn State until after the war. He lettered in '47 and '48 as well as in 1942.

Penn State ended the '42 season with a 6-1-1 log, but as O'Gara quipped, "Post season bowl sponsors are cordially invited to write, wire or phone." No one took O'Gara up on the suggestion.

Pitt won only three games for the third consecutive season. Coach Charles Bowser was replaced by Clark Shaughnessy, who had been voted Coach of the Year in 1940 at Stanford.

1943

Game 43

War Games

The war continued to drag on as President Franklin Delano Roosevelt and Prime Minister Winston Churchill met in Casablanca, Cairo and Teheran to coordinate Allied strategy.

Back in the States, wartime football was taking shape as well. Many military trainees were enrolled in schools throughout the nation. Those who were, benefitted, because all eligibility rules had been lifted. In some instances, seniors from seasons past lined up with teams they had played against in former years.

Penn State had over 2,500 servicemen from the Army, Navy and Air Force on campus in 1943. Most were camped in fraternity houses which the government leased as barracks. Although university officials pushed for the discontinuation of football, Bob Higgins said he'd go with what he had.

The Navy felt strongly that its V-12 trainees would greatly benefit from sports, so they sent Higgins 600 trainees from which he could build his program. No other Penn State coach has ever had such an enormous try-out squad from which to cut.

But the military squad posed another problem for Higgins. He never knew which of his men would be eligible to play, in many cases, until noon on game day. According to the late Penn State historian, Ridge Riley, with all the changes the government made it owed Penn State eight backs, nine linemen, one manager and a scorecard.

Aldo Cenci, Penn State quarterback, 1943.

The 1943 Pitt backfield: Louis Chelko, right halfback; Bill Abromitis, fullback; Frank Knisley, left halfback; and Joe Mocha, quarterback.

Penn State's military defeated Pitt's civilian team, 14-0, at Pitt Stadium for Higgins' third straight win over Pitt. Halfback Bill Abromitis, a Naval trainee, must have felt odd as he had been a Pitt fullback, but was now assigned to Penn State. Because Pitt had been the college of choice when it came time to award varsity letters in 1943, Abromitis received his from Pitt, not Penn State.

If all this sounds a bit weird, consider that it was taking place all over the country at America's institutions of higher learning. For example, Michigan was military, Ohio State, civilian. Schools such as Alabama, Auburn and Kentucky dropped football altogether that year.

But on to the game. Abromitis set up his own touchdown with an 18-yard pass to Dick Trumbull to the Panther 3 in the first quarter. He lost a yard on the next play but finally pushed his way past former Pitt teammate Dick Trachok for the Lion touchdown that made it 7-0, following the PAT.

Penn State scored again two minutes before the half ended when Dick McCown, who had joined the team only three weeks earlier, faked holding a placement on a field goal attempt, and ran for a touchdown.

Ex-Pitt Ace Helps State Defeat Pitt

Pitt, under new head coach Clark Shaughnessy, did nothing right and finished the afternoon with minus 26-yards rushing. It is believed that's the first time in the series either team was held to minus yardage. (Because most newspapers did not publish a statistical breakdown until the '40s, such stats are difficult to determine.)

One last trivia tidbit . . . Ed Czekaj, the man who booted both Penn State extra-points, would later become the school's athletic director.

The experimental season did nothing to help either Penn State or Pitt. The Lions were 5-3-1 under Bob Higgins; Pitt 3-5 under Shaughnessy. The mixture of military and civilians would end midway into the following season.

1944

Game 44

When You Least Expect It

The last thing Penn State anticipated on Nov. 25, 1944 was to lose to Pitt. Hell, for that matter, to get shut out by Pitt. Bob Higgins' Lions had won three games in a row starting with a 41-0 massacre of Syracuse, a 7-6 thriller over Temple and a 34-19 rout of Maryland. They were 6-2. Lowly Pitt was 3-5.

But as you can see from past years, anything could and usually did happen in this series. What was it Alan Funt used to say . . . when you least expect it, you're elected, you're the star today . . . In this case, the star was Pitt freshman Bernie Sniscak, a 160-pound halfback.

Sniscak led the 14-0 upset with a 93-yard kickoff return that gave Pitt all the points it needed. Oddly enough, you won't find Sniscak's feat listed in either Pitt or Penn State record books even though his return is the third longest in series history.

Clark Shaughnessy's troops bit the Lions twice in the third quarter to capture the game before a disappointing crowd of 10,000 at Pitt Stadium. Pitt threatened to score twice in the first quarter but was denied, then staved off two Penn State scoring attempts in the second quarter.

Pitt's other touchdown resulted from an errant Elwood Petchel pass being picked off by Pitt's Loren Braner. His 40-yard return to the Lion 15-yard line left it up to Gene Gaugler to put the finishing touches on the upset with a nine-yard run.

An untimely offsides penalty wiped out the Lions' only score in the fourth quarter with Petchel throwing an end zone completion to Don Miltenberger.

Sniscak's kickoff return, however, took some of the rage out of the Lions' roar in the second half.

Cradling Negley Norton's kick at his 7, Sniscak zig-zagged his way down the field for Pitt's first score. What to this point had been a dull game brought the crowd to its feet and inspired the Panthers the remainder of the way.

Pitt was fortunate to overcome a ridiculous 132 yards in penalties.

Penn State returned to Mt. Nittany wearing scorch marks. The Lions still trailed in the series with 17 wins, five less than Pitt. And, of course, there was still those two 0-0 ties back in the early 20s.

1945

Game 45

Freshman Fury

Wartime football was coming to a close. Germany and Japan had already surrendered. Now it was time for the nation — the world — to pull itself back together.

The ravages of war took their toll on college football, too. It would be some time, years actually, before many schools could restore respectability to their programs. The days of military and civilian football teams were at an end. And isn't it ironic that Army was voted the Number One team in the country in 1944 and 1945?

Look at it this way: America had the best fighting men in the world. Some of those men were playing football in the service. It made sense.

Things were still pretty much in disarray on the campuses of Pitt and Penn State. Pitt fans were yearning for the good old days — the glory days of Pop Warner and Jock Sutherland. Years of three-victory seasons tended to rekindle nostaglia among Panther followers.

Penn Staters didn't have that much to fall back on except a couple of good years with Tom Fennell, Bill Hollenback and Hugo Bezdek. But at least Bob Higgins was returning the Lions to respectability after several shaky years.

One of the fascinating aspects of the Pitt-Penn State series concerns long runs. Either from scrimmage, runbacks or interceptions, long runs always seemed to play a key role in these games.

Including 1945, would you believe that in 19 games in which a

Jimmy Joe Robinson, Pitt back, who holds the record for the longest rushing play in series history — 90 yds. — in 1945.

Clark Shaughnessy, Pitt Head Coach, 1943 to 1945.

Pitt Beats Penn State, 7-0, On Robinson's 90-Yard Run

Panther player rambled 40 or more yards, Pitt won 18? The only loss was in 1941, despite Special Delivery Jones' 40-yard touchdown and 56-yard punt return.

Considering that to this point Pitt had won 26 games in the series, you can clearly see a pattern emerging.

The 1945 contest played in Pitt Stadium was no different. This time the Lion nemesis was halfback Jimmy Robinson from Connellsville, Pa. Robinson tore loose for 90 yards and the game's only touchdown in the first quarter as Pitt spoiled Penn State's bid for a six-win season.

Maybe a 7-0 victory doesn't seem like much, but Clark Shaughnessy's Panthers needed it to finish with a 3-5 record.

What makes Robinson's run all the more special is the fact he was a freshman. Just as frosh Bernie Sniscak had torpedoed the Lions the year before, now it was Jimmy Robinson's crack at first-year immortality.

That's not all. Robinson's run came off as an unusual bit of strategy on Penn State's part. Lion Coach Bob Higgins elected to punt on third down near midfield. If Higgins' plan was to fool Pitt, imagine how shocked he must have been to see Robinson waiting at his own 15 for the ball, then drift back to the 10 where he began his run.

Penn State had two excellent chances to tie, even to win the game. But a second-quarter interception and a stingy Pitt defensive stand in the final quarter quelled all that.

The victory snapped a four-game losing streak for the Panthers but it was not enough to save Shaughnessy's job. After three seasons and a dismal 10-17 record, he was replaced by Wesley Fesler.

Shaughnessy had it coming. He mocked the alumni by dressing Pitt in scarlet during the Panthers' six-game losing streak that season. Also, he had been linked to a scandal which alleged he had connections with pro football.

Like his predecessor, Fesler was just one in a long list of men Pitt looked upon to restore the sacred halo of the past. In reality, that wouldn't happen for decades to come, although one man, John Michelosen, came close toward the end of his coaching career.

1946

Game 46

Abe

You can search all day through the Pitt record book and you won't come across the name of Bill Abraham. He played halfback at Pitt from 1946-49, right after WW II when things were very much unsettled in college football.

He didn't score a whole lot of points or gain thousands of yards like George McLaren and Tony Dorsett. Abe's accomplishments were few at Pitt. It was later when he went into high school coaching that he would leave an indelible stamp on Pennsylvania football.

But in 1946, Bill Abraham completed one chore that led Pitt to a 14-7 victory. He scored a touchdown. For Abe, it was his finest hour in four meetings against Penn State.

The heroics began like this: Penn State halfback Bobby Williams had a pass deflected by Lou "Bimbo" Cecconi just enough to fall into the hands of teammate Bill Bruno at the Panther 36-yard line.

Pitt's march began with Abe dashing for 17 yards and quarterback Carl DePasqua, who would later coach the Panthers, throwing 38 more yards to Cecconi to Penn State's 4-yard line. Abraham tidied things up with a touchdown three plays later, giving Pitt a 7-0 lead.

Pitt made it 14-0 in the fourth quarter when DePasqua threw a seven-yard TD pass to Leo Skladany in the end zone. If Skladany's name sounds familiar, it should. The Skladany family is legend in Pittsburgh. Leo was the brother of another Pitt end, Joe, who played from 1931-33. A third brother, Tom, didn't play football at Pitt, but his

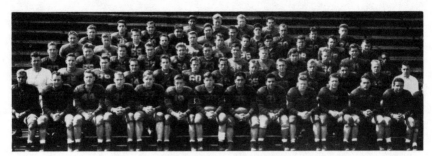

Pitt Varsity squad, 1946.

son, Tom Jr., went on to become one of the nation's best punters at Ohio State.

Penn State closed the gap to 14-7 late in the final quarter when Bob Weitzel finished off a 60-yard drive with a one-yard touchdown that gave the 50,000 who sat in sub-zero temperatures at Pitt Stadium some anxious moments.

But let's get back to Bill Abraham, who would never score another touchdown in the series but would become a household name in Western Pennsylvania.

Abe left Pitt and embarked on a career as a high school coach. In 1956, he took over Hempfield's program near Greenburg, Pa. From 1961 to 1971 Abe had the best winning percentage (.743) in the Western Pennsylvania Interscholastic Athletic League (WPIAL) with a 107-33-4 lifetime record.

Among his accomplishments were four all All-State quarterbacks, including Michigan's Dick Vidmer and Illinois' Bob Naponic, both starters in the Big 10 in 1965.

Once a trim-looking running back, Abe had grown to nearly 300 pounds when he retired in 1971.

"I left because I was tired," he would later say. "I was physically beat, my health was poor and I couldn't take the strain."

For five years, he watched a powerhouse program disintegrate until Abe could take losing no longer. He returned as Hempfield's coach in 1977. The *Pittsburgh Post-Gazette* called it, "The Second Coming of Abraham."

"I came back to give them the leadership they need," Abe explained. "But I can't be the miracle man people think I am." In two years, Abe restored Hempfield to respectability.

In 1977, he was elected the *first* president of the Pennsylvania

151

State High School Football Coaches Association. Even today, Bill Abraham is regarded as a virtual living legend in Western Pennsylvania football.

Finally, Panther Coach Wes Fesler, who replaced Clark Shaughnessy prior to the season, left Pitt for Ohio State where he would later resign, thereby setting the stage for one Wayne Woodrow Hayes in 1951.

1947

Game 47

Higgins' Moment

Bob Higgins had waited 18 years for this moment. Eighteen years to stand up and shout to anyone within hearing distance that his Nittany Lions were undefeated. The best damn football team in the East!

The moment came on Nov. 22, 1947 shortly after Penn State mashed Pitt, 29-0, before 33,000 at Pitt Stadium. In the days ahead, Penn State would receive only its second-ever bowl bid to meet SMU in the Cotton Bowl on New Year's Day.

"An undefeated season is a thing that happens very seldom to any coach," Higgins said of Penn State's 9-0 regular season record. "I don't know about a bowl game. We have several boys and we wouldn't want to play anywhere without them."

Speedy halfback Bobby Williams paced the Lion attack with two touchdowns. Elwood Petchel and Dennie Hoggard each tallied once and Ed Czekaj kicked a field goal and two extra-points.

It all added up to the Lions' first perfect season since going 8-0 under Bill Hollenback. Although Penn State was 7-0-2 in 1920 and 8-0-2 the following year. People were calling this the best season since 1912 because there were no ties.

Williams scored Penn State's first two touchdowns beginning with one run that climaxed a 55-yard drive and another from five yards in the second quarter that gave the Lions a 13-0 lead. Elwood Petchel added a third TD in the third quarter on a 40-yard continuation play. Fullback Fran Rogel blurted through the Pitt line for 20 yards, then quickly lateraled to Petchel who covered the remaining distance, making it 19-0.

A midair recovery of a Pitt fumble by Penn State's Dennie Hoggard, a third string end, gave Penn State its last score in the fourth quarter. Hoggard's run of 20 yards made it 24-0, and Czekaj's field goal at the end was nothing more than trimming on an already decorated tree.

Penn State mortified Pitt in other ways as well. Such as limiting Walt Milligan's Panthers to minus-23 yards rushing and 66 overall. State gained 324 yards on the ground and tacked up 15 first downs. Penn State also set a school record that year by limiting its opponents to just 17 yards rushing per game.

It was Penn State's first victory in Pittsburgh since 1943 and State fans who journeyed west for the game celebrated by tearing down the goalposts and indulging in fistfights over whether it was their right to do so.

Higgins had grown so unaccustomed to post-season play that he said afterward he did not expect a bowl bid.

"I don't even know if we'd want to play a post-season game," he said. "If the college said 'yes' and the boys voted 'yes,' then we might."

As it turned out, Penn State got its bowl bid and ended up tying SMU, 13-13. The game was in jeopardy from the start. There were strong feelings in the southwest about blacks.

The afternoon after Penn State crushed Pitt, SMU Coach Matt Bell assured Higgins that his school would have no objections to playing Penn State in the Cotton Bowl even though the Lions carried three black players—Dennie Hoggard, Larry Joe and Wally Triplett.

Penn State was ranked fourth by the Associated Press in 1947, the first time the school had made AP's Top 10 since the poll began in 1937.

Lions End 1st Perfect Season Since 1912

Williams, Pittsburgh Boy, Tallies Twice in 9th Victory Before 53,000

1948

Game 48

A Little More Time
and . . .

Bob Higgins was beside himself with remorse. He had lost close games to Pitt, twice by seven points in the last three years. But this one hurt even more. It was a gut-wrenching defeat. The kind that leaves a guy feeling he's just had his insides torn out. One minute you're on the brink of doing something terrific, the next, it's over.

For most of the Nittany Lions, the only thing they would remember about this one was the game ended with Penn State on the Panthers' 1-yard line.

"When you lose to a team that played like Pitt today," Higgins said, "alibis are uncalled for. It was tough to lose but you can't complain when you get licked by a team that fights as Pitt did. It's happened to us before, and that's why I never discount a Pitt team on our comparative records."

Pitt tackle Nick Bolkovac intercepted an Elwood Petchel pass in the fourth quarter, then thrilled the 51,075 spectators at Pitt Stadium with a 23-yard touchdown return.

The 7-0 lead, following Bolkovac's own PAT, stood to the end, but Pitt survived two scares.

With Petchel driving the Lions deep into Pitt territory, defender Bobby Lee snared one of Elwood's many late passes on the 5-yard line as the clock had now become a factor. But there was still

Bob Higgins, Penn State Head Coach, 1930 to 1948.

Members of the 1950 Pitt team. From left to right, Nick DeRosa, Bill Gasparovic, Mike Boldin, George Radosevich, Charley Thomas, Nick Bolkovac and Ted Geremsky.

enough time for one more Penn State drive, the one which would test the character of both clubs.

Starting from his 48, Petchel went to the air only to be intercepted again, this time by Jimmy Joe Robinson. But the official on the play ruled pass interference on Robinson, giving Penn State a first down on the Pitt 22 in the final minute.

Petchel completed an 11-yard strike to Larry Cooney for another first down. There were just seconds left. Zip, a nine-yard pass to John Smidansky to the Pitt 2-yard line. Hurry, line-up, only five ticks left and no timeouts.

Petchel crashed to the 1-yard line as the gun sounded. Pitt's line had turned Penn State back. One yard. That's all that separated a loss from a tie. One yard had ruined Penn State's perfect season, breaking a 17-game unbeaten streak.

The Lions closed out 1948 with a 7-0 win over Washington State and 7-1-1 record. Pitt's 6-3 season ended with the Penn State game.

Writers offered Higgins some consolation in holding Pitt to just 65 yards rushing and four first downs. Plus the Lions prevented Pitt from ever crossing the 50 in the first quarter.

This was no consolation to Higgins, however, because in addition to his team's fourth quarter failure, there were two other scoring drives that came up empty in the game.

The first occurred in the second quarter when running back Fran Rogel fumbled the ball away in Pitt territory. The other came in the third quarter after Rogel netted 63 yards on a 67-yard drive with continuous carries, only to be stopped short at the Pitt 16 on fourth down.

Higgins had to give Pitt's line credit. Twice they refused to yield the necessary yardage on fourth down. There were some famous Panthers on that line. Bolkovac, end Leo Skladany, nose guard Don Fisher, and another two-way guard, Bernie Barkouski.

There was no shame in losing to that group of Pitt athletes.

With the loss, Penn State also forfeited a bowl bid despite a 7-1-1 record. Revenge would come, however, four years later when Penn State found Pitt in a similar spot, needing a victory to go to the Orange Bowl.

1949

Game 49

Bimbo Cecconi

Broderick Crawford won an Oscar in 1949 for his superb portrayal of Louisiana's political demagogue, Huey P. Long, in "All the King's Men."

If, perchance, an Academy Award would have been presented for an outstanding performance in one series game between Pitt and Penn State, the Panthers' Lou "Bimbo" Cecconi would have walked away with the nomination that year.

Bimbo scored two touchdowns, passed for another, and defused three Penn State scoring attempts with interceptions as the Panthers walloped their guests 19-0 in Pittsburgh.

You can argue endlessly where Cecconi's place should be among great Pitt ballplayers, but it's easy to say, this was the best two-way performance in the first 50 years of the series. Still, even Bimbo would have admitted that he had a lot of help on those interceptions from his line, particularly, tackles Nick Bolkovac and Bob Plotz and nose guard Bernie Barkouski, all of whom made pests of themselves in front of the Lions' quarterbacks.

Remember also, that even though Carl DePasqua was technically the Panthers' quarterback, Cecconi was equally adept at throwing the ball, as he proved in this game.

Pitt opened a 6-0 forst quarter lead after Cecconi picked off an Owen Dougaherty pass and marched the Panthers 57 yards to their first touchdown. Cecconi threw 19 yards to Armand DiFonso, who battled to the Lion 38-yard line. On first down, DePasqua went outside for three yards, then lateraled to Cecconi, who scampered the remaining distance for the score.

That's all the points which would go up on the board until the third quarter. Panther back Paul Chess rambled 57 yards to State's 8-yard

159

Louis "Bimbo" Cecconi, Pitt's all-purpose back who scored two touchdowns, passed for another and intercepted three passes in the 1949 shutout of Penn State.

"Bimbo" Cecconi as a Pitt assistant coach.

line where Cecconi successfully negotiated an end run making it 13-0.

Cecconi twice intercepted the ball in the fourth quarter and also threw a 58-yard scoring pass to Jimmy Joe Robinson accounting for the final touchdown.

In addition to Cecconi's heroics, the 44,571 in attendance also saw three long yardage plays—38, 57 and 58 yards. It had been eight years since fans were treated to such a smorgasbord of football, going back to 1941 when Penn State's Pepper Petrella scored three touchdowns to outshine Pitt's Special Delivery Jones (one touchdown, two long runs).

The loss was especially hard for one coach. Penn State's Joe Bedenk was making his series debut. His Lions finished up 5-4. Pitt Coach Walt Milligan, who also went by the name Mike, left Pitt after a 6-3 season. His final two years (both 6-3) were the only winning ones in Pittsburgh since 1939.

1950

Golden Anniversary

From Snow to Mud

It figured that when the series finally reached its 50th birthday, Mother Nature would have a helluva cake waiting to greet Pitt-Penn State. Lots of icing. White stuff. That's exactly what she presented in Pittsburgh on Nov. 24, 1950, the day before the game. A record 23 inches of snow paralyzed the city.

Officials twice postponed the game because the snow eventually piled up over two feet in height with more inside Pitt Stadium. Not even a dozen snow plows could have dug the mess out in time. When the game was finally played on Dec. 2 at Forbes Field, only 7,000 braved cold weather to see Penn State shade Pitt, 21-20, on a field of mud.

Pitt, which trailed by as much as 21-7, had a chance to tie the game in the final quarter but kicker Nick Bolkovac's boot sailed wide of the uprights. It was Bolkovac's only missed PAT in 14 attempts that season.

And isn't it ironic that in 1948 it was Bolkovac who had been a hero for the Panthers after he intercepted a pass and ran 23 yards for the game's only touchdown?

Despite all the sludge which blanketed Forbes Field, both teams' combined rushing yardage was 278 and passing yardage 146. The big stat, however, was Pitt being penalized 103 yards to State's 37.

Bill Leonard's sloshing 60-yard interception of a Bob Bestwick pass gave Penn State its first points in the opening minutes of play.

Rip Engle, Penn State Head Coach, 1950 to 1965.

Three passing arms of the Pitt Panthers: Bob Bestwick, Bill Dozinski and Fred Botti, 1950.

The Lions padded the lead to 14-0 at the end of the quarter when Tony Orsini splashed 30 yards to the Pitt 5, then gave way to Paul Anders for the score.

Another Pitt turnover in the second quarter gave the Lions their last touchdown. Pitt's Joe Capp fumbled for the third time in the game and Penn State's Charley Wilson recovered at the Panther 20-yard line. Two plays later, Anders scored again. Vince O'Bara made the crucial extra point. Of course, not even O'Bara had any idea how important that point would be. From the way things appeared on the field, Penn State was going to blow Pitt out and give rookie Coach Rip Engle an early Christmas gift.

A 14-yard touchdown pass from Bestwick to Chris Warriner gave Pitt its first points just 40 seconds before the half ended. The drive covered 75 yards with Bestwick hitting his two favorite receivers, Nick DeRosa and Warriner, on several tries.

Bolkovac's initial conversion was wide but an offsides call against Penn State gave him another chance. He missed again, but the Lions were offsides again. Finally, Bolkovac's third attempt was good and there were no penalties. Score: Penn State 21, Pitt 7.

That touchdown seemed to have provided Pitt with just enough momentum to start the second half in the right frame of mind. Armand DiFonso picked up 43 yards in a 97-yard march which culminated with Bestwick throwing two passes to Warriner for 25 yards and Jim Campbell plunging over from the 1-yard line, to make it 21-14.

By now, the momentum had clearly swung over to the Panthers.

Bill Reynolds kept things going with a 49-yard punt return early in the last quarter to the Penn State 14. Somehow, Reynolds managed to slip past three tacklers while reversing his field. A penalty pushed the ball back to the 25.

On second down, Bestwick dropped back and appeared trapped around the 30-yard line. Suddenly, the Panther quarterback jerked to his left and hurled an off-balance throw to DeRosa in the end zone. DeRosa's fine leaping grab made it a one-point game, 21-20.

Bolkovac's kick was true but Pitt was found to have 12 players on the field. After the additional yardage was tacked on, Bolkovac went through the routine motions, hit the ball, and incredibly, missed everything. Pitt was doomed.

In the closing minutes, Penn State picked off two Bestwick passes to eliminate any danger of Pitt winning the game.

Rip Engle was ecstatic with his young Lions.

"Here's the kind of kids they are," he told reporters. "Last week we stayed three days in Pittsburgh (because of snow) and finally we had to pile everybody in a truck early in the morning and plow through the snow. No one got a bite of breakfast till after 12 o'clock and there wasn't a single squawk.

"This is the greatest bunch of boys I've ever had. Their attitude has been splendid."

Actually, it's not surprising they were Rip's greatest bunch because it was only his *first* season in Happy Valley. This was also a week Rip would never forget. Walking through a blinding snow drift earlier in the week, Rip lost his wallet. Thereafter, he wore a money belt. People used to remark that Rip was holding his pants up when

State Whips Pitt on Muddy Field, 21-20

Bolkovac's Missed Point Costs Tie

he ran off the field clutching the belt after games. Actually, he was protecting the belt. He once admitted he placed as much as $5,000 in the belt on game days. Why?

"In case I might want to buy a car," Rip said without batting an eyelash.

After dropping three of their first four games, the Lions ended the 1950 season 5-3-1.

Pitt, also under a new head coach, Len Casanova, had a disastrous season (1-8) and was outscored 204-99.

"You can't fumble the way we did, have all those penalties, spot a team 21 points and expect too much," Casanova said. "In the second half, our kids came back very well. But I don't think a break came our way."

One year Pitt wins on an interception. Another, Penn State because of a missed extra point. Nick Bolkovac would be inclined to agree that breaks have a way of evening themselves out.

* * *

Pitt still held a decisive lead in the series with 29 victories to Penn State's 19 (two ties). The Panthers also led in scoring after 50 games, 638-483. The Lions were improving, though. They captured five games between 1940-50. The previous decade saw them win just one.

1951

Game 51

Chess Game

During the summer past, Pitt Coach Len Casanova resigned and Athletic Director Tom Hamilton took over as interim coach.

Even though Pitt was still winning the majority of series games, Penn State was slowly becoming more competitive. No longer were the Lions losing by scores such as 34-7, 28-7, 26-0.

Going into the 1951 affair, five of the last seven meetings had been decided by a touchdown or less. Plus, Penn State was showing a string of .500 or better seasons while Pitt fluctuated badly, up one year, down the next.

And though Pitt and Penn State split their last 10 games, you can clearly see just how much State's program was progressing after being down in the late '20s through 1939.

From 1940-50 Penn State won 67 games under three different head coaches — Bob Higgins, Joe Bedenk and Rip Engle. Pitt had gone through four — Clark Shaughnessy, Wes Fesler, Walt Milligan and Len Casanova — but only achieved 36 victories in doing so.

Of course, you can almost always discard statistics when talking about the Pitt-Penn State November showdown. This one, played on Nov. 24, 1951, had a familiar ring to it. The Panthers won, 13-7.

Paul Chess, one of the lesser known Pitt running backs, scored on a 16-yard touchdown run in the fourth quarter which broke a 7-7 stalemate. Thus, Pitt thwarted Penn State's bid for a six-victory season (5-4) while picking up only its third victory. Pitt closed out the

Pitt Beats Penn State, 13-7, On Chess' Late Run for TD

season with its seventh loss the following week in Miami, Fla.

There were two scoring passes in this game. Panther quarterback Bob Bestwick tossed a 32-yarder to Chris Warriner at the end of the second quarter giving Pitt a 7-0 lead. Had Penn State been able to contain Pitt just 20 more seconds, it would have gone to the dressing room with a 0-0 tie.

Twice Pitt muffed chances to open the game up. A first quarter drive which began at the Panthers' own 3-yard line fizzled out at the Lion 14 when, of all things, Pitt lost the ball on downs.

History repeated itself for Pitt in the third quarter when it turned the ball over on downs at the Lion 4. But a botched Penn State punt moments later gave Pitt the ball back at the Lion 17. Paul Blanda's 30-yard field goal attempt, however, was wide.

Penn State got its only touchdown in the last quarter on a nine-yard pass from Bob Szajna to Jesse Arnelle. The PAT tied it, 7-7, until Chess' TD run.

One of the unsung heroes in this game was Panther nose guard Joe Schmidt, who at 203 pounds was one of the heaviest men on the squad. Schmidt received a thunderous ovation from the crowd in Pitt Stadium following an afternoon's work spent mostly in the Penn State backfield. A year later, Schmidt would attain All-America status.

1952

Game 52

Remember '48

Edmund Burke once said you can't plan the future by the past. Then again, Edmund Burke never considered the intense rivalry between Pitt and Penn State, where past wrongdoings were not soon forgotten.

All of which is why Penn State's 17-0 victory over Pitt in 1952 was so comforting for Lion supporters. That victory avenged a prior wrongdoing. In 1948, Pitt knocked the Lions out of bowl contention with a 7-0 win. Penn State knew it would someday return the favor.

This upset victory, before 53,766 at Pitt Stadium, cancelled Pitt's post-season date at the Orange Bowl. What should have been a 7-2 year for rookie Coach Lowell Dawson turned out 6-3 with no door prize.

There were no outstanding plays to write home about but a record was tied. Lion quarterback Tony Rados, a junior from Steelton, Pa., equaled a school record with his ninth touchdown of the season. Shorty Miller first set the mark in 1912, then Elwood Petchel tied it in 1948.

Rados played well against Pitt, completing 11 of 21 passes for 107 yards and scoring one touchdown on a one-yard run.

Halfback Buddy Rowell got the game-winner with a three-yard run in the second quarter. Following Rados' TD in the fourth, which made it 14-0, Bill Leonard kicked a 12-yard field goal to end the scoring.

Both Penn State touchdowns were prearranged through the grace of Philadelphia end Jack Sherry, who twice intercepted Pitt's Rudy Mattoli.

Actually, the key to this game was Pitt's erring ways. Three other times the Panthers let scoring opportunities pass them by with a fumble, interception and failed fourth-down attempt. All the while,

Buddy Rowell, Penn State halfback, 1952.

Pitt was outrushing Penn State, 136-81.

Rados fumbled in the first quarter on his 33, a play which should have sparked Pitt. Instead, the Panthers coughed it up a few plays later.

Pitt marched to the Lion 28 in the second quarter, then lost it on downs . . . marched to the Lion 15 later that quarter, then lost it on an interception. Pitt, in other words, beat itself.

Penn State had gotten revenge and its magic 20th series victory.

The Lions ended up 7-2-1 under Rip Engle, but Pitt drew the post-season honors. Panther fullback Eldred Kraemer and two-way guard Joe Schmidt were selected to the All-America squad. The last Panther to achieve AA status was guard Bernie Barkouski in 1949.

Official Program ● Twenty-Five Cents

NOVEMBER 22, 1952 ● PITT STADIUM

PITT vs

PENN STATE

1953

Game 53

Of Rados and Model-T

The preceding chapter would adequately serve in talking about the 1953 game. The score was the same, as was the man who led Penn State to victory—Tony Rados.

Penn State again finished 6-3. Pitt was having another one of those 3-5-1 years where the best Lowell Dawson could say about his Panthers was they barely broke even in scoring (143-138).

Ah, but the 42,277 who sat in Pitt Stadium got a glimpse of a great running back dressed in Blue and White named Lenny Moore. One of the great injustices was college football's failure to give Moore the proper respect due him.

This was Moore's sophomore season, but by the time he graduated he had rewritten the record books. Some of those records, such as his career, season and game rushing averages, still stand today. Yet Lenny Moore NEVER made All-American.

Moore stunned Pitt with a 79-yard touchdown run that gave Penn State a 10-point first-half lead that only needed a little nursing the rest of the way in the 17-0 shutout.

Pitt defender Henry "Model-T" Ford—honest, that was his name—tied a series and school record with three interceptions. Quick now, who was the man Henry Ford tied? If you answered Lou "Bimbo" Cecconi, you're right. Bimbo snared three out of thin air during a 19-0 Pitt victory in 1949.

Penn State jumped in front 3-0 in the second quarter on a 15-yard field goal by Jim Garrity following a sensational 50-yard pass play from Rados to Bill Straub. Moore's touchdown soon followed for the 10-0 halftime lead.

The Lions took the second half kickoff and drove 63 yards for their final score as Buddy Rowell went off left tackle only a foot from the goal line. Rados' adroit passing accounted for 45 of those 63 yards.

By game's end, the Penn State senior had completed 13 of 25 attempts for 160 yards. Rados' last two games against Pitt are among the best consecutive passing performances in series his-

Penn State Tramples Pitt
As Rados Stars, 17-0

Tony Rados, Penn State quarterback 1952 and 1953.

tory. But that wasn't all that was thrown against Pitt that day. Crateloads of oranges had been brought in anticipation of Pitt's Orange Bowl bid. Annoyed with losing, Pitt fans pelted their team from the stands.

What they didn't know was that Al Michaels had done a terrific scouting job on Pitt and convinced Engle to switch from his usual 5-3-3 defense to a 7-2-2. It left Pitt in bewilderment the entire game and its fans equally unhappy.

By the way, this was Lowell Dawson's final full season at the Pitt helm. Illness caused him to step aside midway into 1954, and Pitt AD Tom Hamilton again came out of his office and onto the field as interim coach.

1954

Game 54

Lenny Moore

This was to be Lenny Moore's "best" effort against Pitt, meager as it may seem when you look at the final totals. There is little question that Moore would have had a better day if the turf at Pitt Stadium were dry, rather than muddy from a steady drizzle.

Pitt held Moore to 68 yards on the ground and also prevented him from scoring a touchdown—the only time that happened in 1954.

When it was over, Penn State had won its third straight series shutout, 13-0, before 47,266 drenched patrons. But less, as the saying goes, is sometimes Moore. Even though the junior halfback from Reading, Pa., didn't have a great game, he did set a new season rushing record and overtake Arizona's Art Luppino as the nation's leading ground gainer that day.

Moore's 68 yards gave him 1,082 on the year, breaking Shorty Miller's 1912 record of 1,031. Moore's single-season total would eventually fall but not his season average, also set in 1954.

That average—8.0 yards per carry—has withstood the challenge of guys like Charlie Pittman, Lydell Mitchell, John Cappelletti and Matt Suhey. Even today, it remains the all-time Penn State standard.

And in case you're wondering, Moore did not win any post-season honors. The Heisman Trophy, you say? It went to Wisconsin's Alan Ameche.

Penn State's quarterbacks set up both touchdowns in the game. Second-string signalcaller Bob Hoffman threw a 19-yard touchdown

Lenny Moore, Penn State halfback.

Lenny Moore, the Baltimore Colt, autographs a football for Johnny Unitas, Jr.

pass to Jack Sherry for the Lions' first score in the second quarter. Sherry's reception was his first scoring pass of the season and it came on an afternoon that was to be his last as a collegian.

In the third quarter, Don Bailey, Penn State's regular quarterback, sneaked over from the 3-yard line to make it 13-0. Penn State's scoring drives were 55 and 56 yards, respectively.

For the remainder of the game, the only question was whether the soggy grass and Pitt's linemen could prevent Moore from attaining 100 yards on the ground. His effort, as it turned out, was the lowest single-game yardage he accumulated in that season.

Moore had rushed for 140 against Penn earlier that season. But Lion Coach Rip Engle is also to blame because he used Moore as a decoy in this game thus limiting his time with the ball. Engle later apologized to Lenny for not allowing him a shot at breaking a few more Eastern rushing records.

"Coach," Moore replied, "I had a wonderful time in there today. Faking is much easier on you."

Two blocked Panther punts in the opening quarter nearly led to Penn State scores but on the first, the Lions negated the turnover with a fumble. On the second blocked punt, Hoffman threw an apparent touchdown to Jesse Arnelle off a fake field goal.

No question, it was a brilliant call by Rip Engle. Only problem was, Arnelle caught the ball outside the end zone.

Pitt never got past Penn State's 40-yard line and twice Moore came up with interceptions as a defensive back. Few people remember that Moore was one of the last great running backs who went both ways on occasion.

Pitt's interim coach, Tom Hamilton, juggled his lineup in an attempt to stave off defeat. He had done the same thing the week before in upsetting Nebraska, 21-7. Pitt's season ended on a sour 4-5 note, as did Hamilton's coaching career. He hired John Michelosen to be his successor in 1955.

When Engle walked into the locker room after the game, someone had scribbled "Seniors 47; Pitt 0" on the blackboard. Engle thought for a moment. Then he realized that his seniors had shut out Pitt three consecutive years.

Engle's 7-2 log wasn't far off the pace set by his 1952 squad, which went 7-2-1. And like that team, Penn State in 1954 still hadn't received a bowl bid, which is doubly unfortunate as most of the nation was never exposed to the running of Lenny Moore, considered by many the greatest running back who ever wore a Penn State jersey.

1955

Game 55

Centennial Snowstorm

Thirteen years had gone by since Penn State last hosted Pitt at Beaver Field. Hosted. That's a bad word to use, because Pitt played so many games on its native soil that even when the Lions got an occasional home game, it was more like tossing Penn State a bone and saying, "Here fellas, we'll let you have this one." Then another decade or two of Panther home games would follow.

So it would be wrong to characterize any series games in State College as being "hosted." "Permitted" would be a better word, a more precise choice.

Students in State College had been celebrating the school's centennial. When chartered in 1855, Penn State taught more than just the arts and sciences. It was founded primarily to offer rural students a background in agriculture and the so-called mechanical arts of farming.

Students were required to perform physical labor "no less than three hours daily," according to the biography that appears in the Penn State media guide. Included among the laborious chores were "cutting wood, picking up stones, and chasing cows and pigs."

And you probably thought the only things boys at Penn State— which was listed in *Playboy* among the nation's best "party schools" of the '70s—did was attend frat parties, drink beer and chase nubile, young women.

Whatever, in this game, Penn State's football team was left chasing Pitt's runners in a blinding snowstorm that left both teams wearing white and over six inches on the ground. After not having scored a point against a Rip Engle unit in three years, Pitt exploded for 20.

It's hard to imagine how Pitt could have won 20-0 when Lenny Moore was in there, but the Lion senior gained only 13 yards on 10 carries that day, one of his worst performances in college ball.

The snow blanketed the field so well, yard lines and hash marks were impossible to locate which, in part, helps explain how Pitt quarterback Pete Neft, who scored one touchdown, could successfully pick up 35 yards on "sneak" plays. The leading snow blower was Panther halfback Lou Cimarolli (70 yards).

Corny Salvaterra, who started at quarterback against Penn State in 1954, was benched, and resurfaced a year later as a back-up, had the game's biggest play, a 62-yard touchdown with 2 minutes, 30 seconds left that made it 20-0.

Second-string fullback Bobby Grier scored the middle touchdown to cap off a 77-yard drive.

The first quarter was a scoreless duel, but Pitt got the only points it needed in the second on Neft's dive over the middle from less than a yard out. The drive was only 32 yards because Lion quarterback Milt Plum tried a long pass at Pitt's 39 only to be intercepted by Grier. Were it not for Moore, Pitt would have scored sooner.

There was no denying Grier his touchdown in the third quarter, however. After Penn State managed to blow a fourth-down-and-inches play at the Panther 22, Pitt drove 77 yards out of a T-formation for a 14-0 lead, with Grier scoring on a two-yard run.

Salvaterra's long TD run got an able assist from Moore, who dropped a pitchout at the Panther 34. Three downs later, Salvaterra slithered through the right side of the Pitt line, swerved past two linebackers, shook off another tackle, and outran Moore and Billy Kane for the touchdown.

It was a depressing way for Moore to end his collegiate career. Lenny left behind several Nittany Lion records which were quoted earlier. He is also fourth in all-purpose yardage with 3,332 (2,380 rush, 89 pass, plus 863 return). Lenny Moore played his entire pro career with the Baltimore Colts and was named to the Professional Hall of Fame at Canton, Ohio, in 1975.

The 20-0 victory was the first for Pitt Coach John Michelosen against Rip Engle, and along with it came a bid to the Sugar Bowl. Georgia Tech won 7-0 but Pitt's 7-4 record was the best in Western Pennsylvania since Jock Sutherland's 8-2 finish in 1938.

1956

Game 56

From Oranges to Plums

There hadn't been a tie in the series since 1921 when neither team scored for the second year in a row.

Pitt came into this game with a 6-2 record and visions of the Orange Bowl. Penn State just wanted to play the spoiler role. In a way, the Lions spoiled things for Pitt, but not quite as effectively as they had wanted.

Pitt didn't get the Oranges but settled for a rematch against Georgia Tech in the Gator Bowl, where the Panthers lost 21-14.

Penn State's fine senior quarterback, Milt Plum, who was destined to have a creditable career with the Cleveland Browns and Detroit Lions, missed a 24-yard field goal in the last minute, thereby preserving a 7-7 tie.

Plum had a stellar performance in front of 51,123 at Pitt Stadium completing nine of 13 passes for 118 yards as well as calling the defensive signals for the Lions. He did not enter the game until the second quarter when Penn State's scoring drive was already in progress under the guidance of starting quarterback Al Jacks, who normally was Plum's understudy.

After stopping a Pitt drive at the 1-yard line, Jacks took the Lions to the Pitt 34 behind the fleet-footed running of Bruce Gilmore, who was being touted as "the next Lenny Moore." Plum entered the game at the start of the second quarter and immediately fired an 11-yard pass to Les Walters, then sent Billy Kane through the line for nine more. Plum squeezed out two more yards to the Panther 12.

Kane and Ray Alberigi, one of Rip Engle's many halfbacks, traded handoffs as Penn State took it to the 3. Kane went over for the touchdown and it was 7-0 following Plum's conversion. Overall, the drive covered 60 yards in frigid weather that made passing the ball nearly as difficult as catching it.

Pitt's Dick Bowen took Plum's kickoff and returned it 23 yards to start a 75-yard scoring drive. Jim Theodore's 28 yards plus Bowen's 18 accounted for the significant chunks of real estate that advanced the ball to the Penn State 18.

Quarterback Corny Salvaterra faked a handoff that drew the linebackers up, then faded right and threw across the middle to Michael Rosborough. Rosy made a fine catch in the end zone and Ambrose Bagamery nailed the all-important PAT to tie the game, 7-7.

On that pass play, Engle ordered Pitt's All-American end Joe Walton double covered. Walton had to live with that coverage the rest of the afternoon, which must have been upsetting—he failed to catch any passes for the first time that season.

Both teams showed signs of breaking this one open as the game progressed but costly fumbles, penalties or stout defenses deflated anyone's chance of doing so. Salvaterra nearly lost the game for Pitt late in the fourth quarter when he foolishly elected to swipe at a punt which was over his head, got spun around, and was tackled inches from his own end zone. Pitt spent four downs just trying to prevent a safety before punting it out of harm's way.

Penn State had the best opportunity to win it that quarter on Plum's field goal attempt, but the ball was wide of the uprights.

The Lion's season ended with a 6-2-1 record. Pitt went on to defeat Miami before losing to Georgia Tech in the Gator Bowl.

1957

Game 57

Best Available Toe

Soccer-style kickers made a big splash in college football in the '70s. But believe it or not, some teams were toying with the idea of using soccer players for extra points and field goals as far back as the late '50s. Ask any student of Pitt-Penn State football lore who the first soccer-style kicker was in this series and chances are, he'll say the Lions' Alberto Vitiello.

Vitiello virtually rewrote the kicking records at Penn State between 1970 and '72, only to watch them fall to a newer generation of soccer type kickers (Chris and Matt Bahr).

Although Vitiello isn't a bad guess, it's not the right answer. As far as it can be determined, the first immigrant soccer-style kicker to make an appearance in the series was Pitt's Norton Seaman in 1957. Seaman was an East Indian who played soccer prior to immigrating to the United States.

And on Nov. 23 of that year, Norton Seaman made himself a rather popular fellow in Pittsburgh by kicking the deciding point in Pitt's 14-13 victory before 45,760 at Pitt Stadium.

Talk about being cool under pressure—Seaman was forced to boot the winning point twice. Although his first kick was good, Pitt was offsides. After the penalty was marched off, Seaman again slammed the ball through the goalposts for the winning edge. His extra point nullified Penn State's chances for a Gator Bowl bid.

What surprised people about this game was how Pitt was able to

Norton Seaman, Pitt's first soccer-style kicker.

overcome a 13-point deficit when, for three quarters, they were pushed about the field like tackling dummies.

Two native Pittsburghers, sophomore Eddie Caye and junior Al Jacks, gave Penn State its 13-0 lead beginning in the second quarter. Penn State faced a fourth down situation at the Pitt 2-yard line when quarterback Caye admittedly concocted a "homemade" play. Trapped by three Pitt defenders at the 5, Caye spun off a tackle and fired a tracer bullet to senior end Ron Markiewicz, who was barely across the goal line when he caught the ball. Babe Caprara hit the point-after for a 7-0 Lion lead.

Coach Rip Engle inserted Jacks as the Lions' quarterback in the final two periods. Jacks climaxed a 36-yard drive with a nine-yard scoring pass to Paul North, making it 13-0. Caprara's kick was wide left, though. It would make the difference at the end.

Pitt made its charge early in the last quarter. Again, it was left to a quarterback to get something on the board. Junior Bill Kaliden rifled a 22-yard pass to Dick Scherer to set up Fred Riddle's two-yard plunge that made it 13-7.

Three minutes later, Kaliden hit Scherer with the game's long gainer, a 45-yard pass that sent the Pitt end into the end zone, tying the game 13-13. Pitt Coach John Michelosen elected not to use Ivan Toncic for the extra point even though he had successfully kicked Pitt's first conversion.

Instead, Michelosen motioned for Norton Seaman, a third-string guard, to kick the winning point through.

The series finally had a new hero and Pitt fans were able to forget that back in 1950, Nick Bolkovac missed an extra point that would have tied a game against Penn State.

Welcome to Pitt-Penn State football, Norton.

1958

Game 58

No Sophomore Jinx for Lions

Perhaps it was fitting that the underclassmen were coming up with the big plays, the long gainers, the timely catches in the series. Too often, the focus had centered on a senior quarterback or half-back. Let the kids have their fun, too.

And so it came to be in 1958 when Penn State's wily trio of sophomores—Dick Hoak, Don Jonas and Jimmy Kerr—put their combined talents together in the final 30 minutes as the Lions erased a two-touchdown deficit and shocked the Panthers, 25-21, ruining the city of Pittsburgh's 200th anniversary.

After being held to just 12 yards rushing in the first half, the Lions took advantage of two Panther fumbles and converted them into second-half touchdowns. Trailing 13-0 in the third period, Penn State took over at the Pitt 25 after a wobbly snap from center to punter Mike Ditka forced the Panther end to eat the ball.

Quarterback Richie Lucas, who set a series record in the game with a 63-yard punt (later broken in 1965), jogged 18 yards to within two yards of the goal line. Pat Botula then sliced the deficit to 13-6. Penn State attempted a two-point conversion, something new to the game in 1958, but failed.

Andy Stynchula recovered a Pitt fumble at the Panther 32 on the next series as Penn State smelled a rally. Seven plays into the drive,

Richie Lucas, Penn State All-American quarterback, 1958.

Penn State Roars From Behind
In 2d Half to Startle Pitt, 25-21

Hoak threw nine yards to Norm Neff for a touchdown that cut Pitt's lead to one point. Again, Lion Coach Rip Engle, being a daring sort of chap, elected to try a two-point conversion. Again, the pass failed.

Pitt awakened from this nightmare with a 52-yard touchdown run by Chuck Reinhold that gave the Panthers a little more breathing room, 21-12, following Norman Seaman's third successful PAT.

A 50-yard TD run by quarterback Ed Sharockman in the first quarter plus a three-yard run by halfback Joe Scisly had given Pitt a 14-0 first-half cushion.

Now, with a 21-12 lead, the Panthers must have felt they had regained control of the game and to some extent, their own fortunes, for a Cotton Bowl invitation was riding on this game.

Too bad that didn't wash with Penn State's sophomores. There was less than a full quarter to play when the kids grabbed destiny by the throat and suffocated it. Lion quarterback Al Jacks passed nine yards to Neff, chopping the lead down to 21-18.

The clock was ticking down to six minutes as Penn State began its final scoring drive. Kerr, the little speedster from Ohio, hauled down a punt on his own 29-yard line and darted 43 yards to the Panther 28. Hoak, who would have a long career with the Pittsburgh Steelers, took a pitchout from Jacks, ran to one sideline, found nothing there, reversed his field and rambled to the 9 before being stopped.

Time to break one last sophomore jinx. Jacks faked a handoff up the middle to his fullback, Botula, and instead gave the ball to Jonas, who slanted to the left corner of the end zone for the stunning score. Realizing that three prior two-point pass conversions had not worked, Engle took no chances in allowing Pitt to tie this one with a field goal. Jonas was ordered to kick the PAT—which he did. It ended 25-21, Penn State.

The Lions were 6-3-1 and knocked Pitt (5-4-1) out of bowl contention. Engle remarked afterward that he wished he could celebrate William Pitt's bicentennial bash every year.

1959

Game 59

Vitamin C Attack

You never know what to expect when Pitt and Penn State meet. The scale ranges from exultation to chaos, usually in the same day.

Armed with All-American quarterback Richie Lucas, the Lions stalked into Pitt Stadium with a bowl bid already agreed upon and an 8-1 record, its best showing in 12 years. Pitt was only 5-4 even though there were some eye-opening victories over UCLA, Duke and Notre Dame, just the week before.

So what happened? Pitt rambled to a 22-7 victory. Even more embarrassing was Panther kicker Fred Cox dashing 86 yards for a touchdown. Fred Cox, for cripes sake. Who the hell is Fred Cox, besides being a freshman? In time, the world would come to know Fred Cox as one of the NFL's premier kickers with the Minnesota Vikings.

Actually, Cox formed part of Pitt's deadly Vitamin C complex of Cox, Bob Clemens and Jim Cunningham. The trio wreaked havoc on every opponent. Needless to say, it wasn't healthy to face them.

Cox led the Panthers with a touchdown and two PATs, Clemens scored once and so did Ivan Toncic. Pitt's defense yielded only one touchdown, that to Dick Pae, and also sacked Lucas in the end zone for a safety.

Penn State was still feeling the after-effects of a two-point loss to Syracuse, so you can presume this one left the Lions reeling, even though they had a Dec. 19 engagement in Philadelphia (Liberty

Fred Cox, Pitt halfback — kicker, 1959.

Penn State Head Coach, Rip Engle, along the sidelines, 1959.

Pitt Rocks Penn State as Cox Goes 86 for TD

Bowl) with Alabama.

It's ironic, but had Penn State not held the Panthers at bay from the Lion 1-yard line, Lucas never would have gotten himself into that mess, which gave Pitt an early 2-0 lead. Pitt next took the kick, drove 40 yards and scored on quarterback Toncic's one-yard run.

Clemens slipped off right tackle for a 35-yard touchdown run the following quarter, then Cox surprised everyone with a twisting, turning sideline run of 86 yards in the third quarter that made it 22-0.

By then, Lion Coach Rip Engle, who had instructed school officials not to mention the Liberty Bowl invitation until *after* the Pitt game, must have felt fortunate that he already had a bowl bid tucked away. Engle had really been hoping his club would get an Orange Bowl invite to match against the Liberty Bowl bid.

Besides, who wants to play in frosty Philadelphia in December when they can mosey on down to the beach after Orange Bowl practice for a week?

The Lions averted a shutout late in the third quarter by recovering a Pitt fumble and traversing 27 yards for a touchdown behind its second string. Halfback Dick Pae scampered nine yards for the score.

For the third straight time Lucas failed to break the hex that Pitt Stadium held on him. He completed only four of 13 passes and had thrown one interception. Toncic was 3-for-4, but that wasn't anything to get excited about. Of course, Ivan the Terrible did score a touchdown, so he had a slight edge there.

Cox carried the ball 12 times for 129 yards, Clements 16 for 102 and Cunningham 20 for 57. All told, the Panthers clawed their way to 330 yards on the ground.

Pitt finished 6-4; Penn State nipped Bear Bryant's boys on a fake field goal at the Liberty bowl to finish 10th in the UPI poll with a 9-2 record. Richie Lucas was later named to the All-American team.

1960

Game 60

Cox Kick Not Enough

Though the respective records of both teams would lead you to believe otherwise, the 1960 meeting was built around the antici-pated showdown between the passing of Dick Hoak and running of Jimmy Kerr vs. the kicking of Fred Cox and punishing play of Pitt's All-American two-way end, Mike Ditka. Forget that Penn State was 6-3 and Pitt 4-2-3. Bitter rivals never look at each other's records; only the final score.

For 45 minutes Pitt clutched a 3-0 lead to its bosom, the slender thread having been provided in the first quarter on Cox' 35-yard field goal. Now Pitt was marching 78 yards, rattling off 21 straight plays deep inside Penn State territory . . . until Don Jonas intercepted an Ed Sharockman pass on the 8-yard line and returned it to the Lion 27.

Five plays later, Butch Hall bootlegged to his right and threw a nifty 30-yard spiral to Kerr for a 6-3 fourth-quarter edge from which the Lions would build upon, ever so slightly.

The touchdown took some of the steam out of Pitt and was never more evident than on the next Panther drive when Sharockman futilely attempted to spark his troops. Cox punted 40 yards from the Panther 42 and that set the stage for Penn State's last score.

Eight plays into the drive, Penn State was slamming down the door on the Panther 3-yard line. Hoak rolled out to his right on fourth-and-goal and lofted a pass into the beckoning arms of Bob

Richie Lucas (right) and Galen "Butch" Hall, Penn State quarterbacks, 1960.

Mitinger. Dave Hayes ran for the two-point conversion. Penn State had it locked up, 14-3.

Hall threw another scoring pass minutes later to Kerr but it was called back because center Jay Huffman had been an ineligible receiver down field on the play.

Sharockman and David Kraus alternated at quarterback during the waning minutes as Pitt filled the autumn air with aerials, advancing to the Lion 20 before Sharockman was sacked, ending Pitt's only chance for a touchdown.

Pitt had failed to spring Mike Ditka free enough times to hurt Penn State with its double wing formation. What had been billed as a great defensive game—with Pitt supposedly doing all the defensive work—also failed to materialize. Penn State rushed through Ditka's boys for 217 yards (Pitt had 157). The passing stats were nearly equal. Pitt's two quarterbacks threw for 70 yards and Penn State's for 63.

The Liberty Bowl folks were so impressed with the way Rip Engle made a fool out of Bear Bryant in '59 they invited him back in '60 to play Oregon. The Lions gobbled up the Ducks, 41-12, to complete their 7-3 year.

As for the series, neither Engle nor Panther Coach John Michelosen seemed able to get a firm grip on this bitter rivalry. Both schools traded wins from 1957-60. Pitt won in '55, Michelosen's rookie season, but tied in '56.

After 60 meetings, it looked as though no one was going to dominate for any length of time (such was not the case, as we shall see). Pitt continued to pace the series with 33 victories. Penn State had 24 and there were three ties. Pitt was equally superior in the scoring department: 738-603.

1961

Game 61

Trophies and Bowls

The Lambert Trophy, awarded annually to the Eastern football's best team, had become far more controversial than coveted by now. As an illustration of the point, we turn back to 1959 when Yale and Navy shared co-honors. Yale was furious, causing *Philadelphia Daily News* writer Larry Merchant to write that Yale equated victories over West Chester, Wagner and Humboldt State as being on a par with Navy victories over SMU, Air Force and Notre Dame.

The Lambert people decided to alter the wording on future trophies, eliminating the word "championship" and replacing it with "performance." But who's to say what constitutes a best performance?

Penn State clobbered Pitt 47-26 in 1961 in the series' highest scoring game (back then, anyway) and finished the regular season with a 7-3 record. Rutgers had gone a perfect 9-0. The *New York Herald Tribune* said the "honorable" thing to do was award the Lambert Trophy to Rutgers. Alas, it went to Penn State on the basis of a tougher schedule, causing Rutgers Coach John Bateman to whine, "The trophy was supposed to go to the team with the best record, wasn't it?"

Well, do you really think Rutgers could have beaten Penn State in 1961?

Certainly, Pitt thought it could and actually came into the game only a slight underdog despite its horrendous 3-6 record. After a so-

Galen Hall, Penn State quarterback, holds the series record for cumulative yards, 266—gained in the 1961 game.

Hall Tabs 2, Hurls 2 as State Pounds Pitt, Earns Bowl Bids

so first half after which Penn State led 19-14, the Lions tore the flesh off the Panthers' backs in the final two quarters, outscoring their hosts 28-12.

Senior quarterback Galen (Butch) Hall threw touchdown strikes of 23 and 48 yards to Al Gursky and Junior Powell, plus ran for two more. By the game's end, Hall had completed 11 of 14 passes for a series record 256 yards. His cumulative total of 266 yards still stands today. (The single-game passing total was broken in 1972 by John Hufnagel.) Overall, Penn State outgained Pitt, 439 yards to 297, while running off 76 plays to Pitt's 56.

"I was surprised that Penn State was so good," understated Panther Coach John Michelosen.

The game was a 40-14 rout in the fourth quarter before Pitt managed to score two more touchdowns. One was a 49-yard run by fullback Rick Leeson and the other a six-yard TD pass from Jim Traficant to Steve Jastrzembski.

Panther punter Fred Cox had his first attempt blocked at his 14-yard line in the opening quarter and Penn State's Hall turned the miscue into six points. Pitt tied the score 7-7 on Paul Martha's eight-yard pass to John Jenkins minutes later after Martha galloped 60 yards with the ensuing kick.

Hall answered that score with passes of 34 and 22 yards to his end, Jim Schwab, before Buddy Torris fell over from the 1 for a 13-7 lead. Hall muffed the snap on the PAT, however. That goof helped Pitt take the lead as Leeson ran five yards for his first touchdown of the game. Cox kicked, and it was 14-13, Pitt.

A fumble by Pitt's John Telesky set up Penn State's final score in the opening 30 minutes as Hall completed his 23-yard TD strike to Gursky giving the Lions a 19-14 lead.

With the Gator Bowl people looking on, the Lions performed a dazzling second-half show. They opened the third quarter with a 61-yard drive that culminated with Hall's 26-yard pass to Roger Kochman and his own 11-yard scoring run. Kochman's two-point conversion saw State open up a 27-14 lead.

The gap widened to 33-14 on an eight-yard TD run by Kochman, then ballooned to 40-14 on Gursky's four-yard plunge in the final quarter. Hall also threw his 48-yard scoring pass to Powell that quarter.

If the Lambert Trophy wasn't enough of a mess for Penn State, the Gator Bowl bid got sticky, too. The Gator people originally

Paul Martha, Pitt halfback, 1961.

intended to invite Maryland, but the Terps lost the same weekend as Penn State's victory over Pitt. But Rip Engle already hinted that Penn State was thinking Bluebonnet Bowl. Then there was the Gotham bowl, which also wanted Penn State.

Penn State eventually decided on the Gator Bowl, where it humbled Georgia Tech, 30-15. Maryland Coach Tom Nugent, feeling he got the shaft from Engle, was heard to mutter, "Something very funny happened to us on our way to the Gator Bowl."

1962

Game 62

Liske and the Coogan Award

Pete Liske was just a sophomore second-string quarterback when the 1962 season began. Upon its completion, he was Rip Engle's starter and holder of three single-season Penn State records: Most touchdown passes, 12; yards passing, 1,047, and total offense, 1,312. The records have since been broken.

Liske completed eight-of-18 passes for 136 yards and two touchdowns as Penn State blanked Pitt, 16-0 at Pitt Stadium for its first series shutout since 1954. The Pittsburgh Curbstone Coaches' Association named Liske its first recipient of the James H. Coogan Memorial Award as the game's outstanding player. The Coogan award, which has become an annual tradition, is named after the former Penn State sports information director who died in the spring of '62.

Penn State blew into Pittsburgh on Nov. 24 with an 8-1 record and seemed unbothered—for a change—by Pitt having defeated the likes of California, Baylor, UCLA, Syracuse and Army. Recall, this was one of Pitt's better squads despite its season-ending 5-5 record. Panther Coach John Michelosen had Fred Mazurek at quarterback and two outstanding backs in Rick Leeson and Paul Martha.

No big deal. Liske disposed of them with two quick aerials. A 56-yard scoring pass to Roger Kochman in the third quarter and a highly-controversial 18-yard bullet to Al Gursky in the fourth period. Just enough to ensure another Lambert Trophy as Beast of the East.

Liske confined most of his passing heroics to the third quarter. Ron Coates had already given Penn State a 3-0 advantage late in the second quarter. With the ball at the Lion 44, Liske passed to Kochman, who was running a sideline pattern. Kochman caught the ball on the dead run at midfield, shook off Martha, and needed only a block by Dick Anderson at the Panther 30 to score. That made it 10-0 following Coates' extra point.

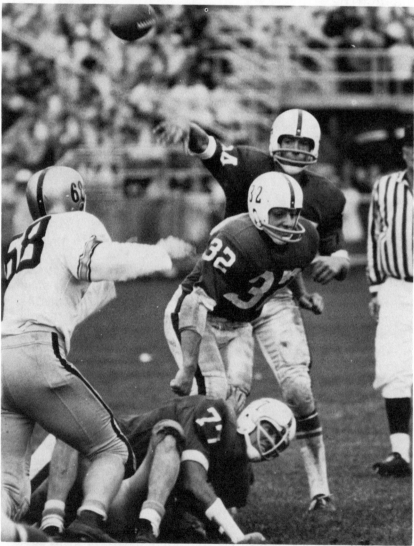

Pete Liske, Penn State quarterback, won the first James H. Coogan award, 1962.

The next Liske touchdown, however, sparked a controversy that made Michelosen, among others, blow his stack. Penn State was only 18 yards from the goal line in the fourth quarter. Lion halfback Al Gursky was being shadowed on the coverage by Pitt's Ed Clark. Clark pushed his way in front of Gursky and made a waist-high interception in the end zone. Almost immediately, Gursky somehow managed to steal it back. Touchdown, Penn State, 16-0.

Michelosen disputed the snatch-catch on two fronts. First, the Pitt coach claimed Liske released the ball past the line of scrimmage. He also claimed Gursky had regained possession off Clark while out of bounds in the corner of the end zone. The officials denied both appeals.

Penn State's biggest problem that afternoon was not on the football field but in the dressing room after the game, when the players were asked to convey their feelings about a bowl game. Nowadays players have little say about bowl games because of the tremendous amounts of money dangled in front of schools. Millions of dollars. Sure, teams go through the ritual of having their players vote, but even if they said "no" to a bowl game, they'd be playing just the same come the end of December or New Year's Day. There's just too much money involved to turn most bowls down.

But back in '62, and in other years as well, the players had a commanding edge over the university when it came time to decide what bowl—if any—they would play in. Engle's 1962 squad was divided over playing in ANY bowl. The seniors participated in the 1960 Liberty Bowl, the '61 Gator Bowl and now were being asked about whether they'd like to go back to the Gator against Florida.

These upperclassmen were adamant in their refusal to play another bowl game. They wanted to spend the holidays with their relatives and girlfriends. According to *Philadelphia Inquirer* reporter John Dell, a bloc of sophomores and key seniors swayed the vote just enough for acceptance of the Gator Bowl bid.

Maybe Penn State would have been better off staying home. Florida won 17-7 and everyone had a pretty miserable time. Because blacks were not allowed in the hotels in Jacksonville, Penn State players were forced to take accommodations in St. Augustine, which was rather removed from the Gator goings-on. It was just like the 1948 Cotton Bowl when Bob Higgins' troops arrived in Texas and found a bunch of restrictions given to them regarding their black players. It was ugly then and the Gator Bowl experience was like reliving a bad dream. But this was America and bigotry, unfortunately, was part of the game plan.

1963

Game 63

A Leader is Slain; Some Games Postponed

John F. Kennedy had been dead less than 48 hours, the fourth American President to be gunned down in our history. Saturday, Nov. 23, 1963 had been set aside as the nation's official day of mourning. Most sporting events came to a halt, either through postponement or cancellation.

The Pitt-Penn State game, scheduled for Nov. 23, 1963, was postponed until Dec. 7 at Pitt Stadium.

Panther quarterback Fred Mazurek, playing with a painful hip injury, inflicted the most damage as Pitt came from behind to win 22-21, in what is generally acknowledged as the best game played between these two titans during the '60s. Mazurek chalked up 142 yards rushing; completed 7 of 15 passes for 108 more (250 total yards) and directed the winning drive which concluded with his 17-yard rollout touchdown. Penn State kicker Ron Coates missed a 27-yard field goal in the final 1 minute, 34 seconds. The kick was long enough but, wide to the left by less than a foot.

Mazurek's performance, the best since 1961 when the Lions' Butch Hall amassed 266 yards against Pitt, overshadowed Penn

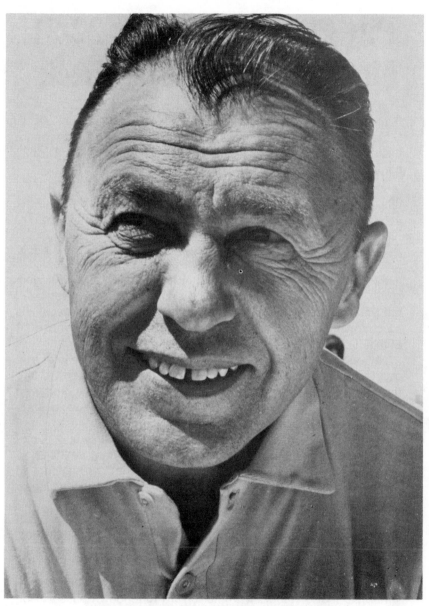

John Michelson, Pitt Head Coach, 1955 to 1965.

Pitt Clips Penn State, 22-21; Mazurek Spurs Comeback

State's Pete Liske, whose own brilliance was without question. Liske, who was drafted by the Eagles that year, completed 11 of 23 passes for 173 yards and two touchdowns.

John Michelosen's Panthers came into the game ranked third and fourth in the polls with an 8-1 record. Lion Coach Rip Engle was pleased his club (7-2) was able to give Pitt a battle. As it was, no team outside the East defeated either Pitt or Penn State that year.

"I've never been prouder of a team than I am of this one," Engle said. "If Pitt is as good as they say, then we're right with them . . ."

Penn State led 7-0 in the first quarter following Gary Klingensmith's nine-yard touchdown. Klingensmith, incidentally, was deaf, but that didn't prevent him from becoming a reliable halfback. His touchdown was preceded by Ed Stuckrath blocking a Panther punt at the Pitt 17-yard line.

Although the Lions held up against a 58-yard Pitt drive later that quarter, they could not stop Pitt's 46-yard drive that extended into the second period. All-American halfback Paul Martha scored from the one but Pitt's two-point pass conversion failed, leaving State with a 7-6 lead.

Mazurek fumbled on Pitt's next possession, his only faux pas of the afternoon, and Penn State recovered at the Panther 35. Liske took over from there and on the seventh play of the drive hit tight end Jerry Sandusky with a nine-yard touchdown pass, giving the Lions a 14-6 lead.

Panther fullback Rick Leeson pulled Pitt to within 14-12 at the half with a one-yard TD following a 34-yard reception from Mazurek. Leeson later missed a 37-yard field goal, but his 35-yard boot in the third quarter catapulted Pitt ahead, 15-14.

Liske answered that three-pointer immediately, engineering a 74-yard drive that climaxed with his 10-yard touchdown pass to Don Caum, who made a sensational end zone reception for a 21-15 Lion advantage. Almost unnoticed among the rave reviews of Mazurek and Liske was Caum's total of 99 yards receiving (four passes).

The 21-15 lead should have held, except Michelosen was forced to sit Mazurek for the final five minutes of the quarter. The hip-pointer was acting up. Mazurek, however, insisted on returning to action.

With 52,349 looking on, Mazurek re-entered the game in the last quarter and directed Pitt to a thrilling 77-yard drive that ended with his own touchdown. In all, Mazurek had carried the ball 23 times in pain. His 250 yards that day were second only to the 295 he piled up against Miami the week before.

There is no question this was John Michelosen's greatest Pitt club. But miscarriages of justice are well documented in sports and Pitt, despite a 9-1 record, failed to get a single bowl bid. It was crazy. Teams had gone to bowls with two and three losses every year. There is ample reason to suspect this was another in what would be a series of bowl misgivings involving that famed controversy surrounding the so-called "myth about Eastern football."

What more could the bowl people want? Pitt shut out UCLA 20-0, beat Washington 13-6, slaughtered California 35-15, edged Syracuse 35-27, rolled over Notre Dame 27-7 and topped Miami 31-20. And then defeated Penn State for added measure.

Martha and tackle Ernie Borghetti won first team All-America honors. Pitt was ranked fourth by the AP and third by UPI.

Michelosen was bitterly disappointed. Here he was in his finest hour at Pitt with nothing to show for it except a 9-1 record and no recognition. Two years later, he would be fired.

Researcher Randy L. Jesick analyzed Michelosen's 1963 team a decade after that season. What he found is still considered simply astonishing. Michelosen was known for being a rigid coach at Pitt. But few probably ever gave him credit for being a man who demanded excellence from his players in the classroom, too.

Of the 75 players on his roster, Jesick found that 66 had graduated; 33 from that lot enrolled in post-graduate programs. There were three doctors, 15 dentists, five lawyers, seven educators, 28 involved in industry and two ministers.

Jesick concludes his report by noting that the starting 11 (all white) each found a prosperous job. "They were winners in the game of football," Jesick wrote, "and now they're winners in the game of life."

1964

Game 64

A Visit to Beaver Stadium

At University Park, on Nov. 21, Penn State hosted Pitt at Beaver Stadium—the Lions' first home game against their arch rival since 1955. Following the 1959 season, the steel structure comprising Beaver Field was dismantled and moved in 700 pieces one mile east to its present location. Although Penn State had been playing home games at its new facility for four years, Pitt did not make its first appearance at Beaver Stadium until 1964.

A record 50,170 showed up on Nov. 21 as Penn State shut out Pitt 28-0, the Panthers' worst defeat since a 35-0 loss to Syracuse in 1959. The loss was also Pitt's worst series defeat since 1947 when the Panthers were held scoreless, 29-0.

Lion fullback Tom Urbanik, a draftee of the Washington Redskins, carried the ball 20 times for 107 yards and two touchdowns before leaving the game at the end of the third quarter with an ankle sprain.

As usual, the Lions were apprehensive approaching their final game of the season. Pitt might have been 3-4-2, but it had crushed Army and came within a missed one-yard field goal of upsetting Notre Dame (17-15).

Plus, the memory of Freddy Mazurek's destructive forces of 1963 still lingered in players' minds. Mazurek had a new weapon, too, in

Penn State Head Coach Rip Engle (right) and his assistant, Joe Paterno, 1964.

sophomore speedster Eric Crabtree. So even though the Lions were 5-4, Rip Engle advised them of that old adage, "When you least expect it . . ."

What Pitt didn't expect was Penn State limiting Mazurek, the Panthers' dashing rollout quarterback, to just 28 yards on the ground and 36 in the air. Crabtree was also held in check with a meaningless 10 yards on as many carries.

The Lions stockpiled 326 yards overall and 28 first downs compared to Pitt's embarrassing 100 and eight, respectively.

Urbanik, who hailed from Donora, Pa., and somehow eluded John Michelosen's recruiting grip, ran from four different formations in this game and was voted the James H. Coogan Memorial Award as MVP. Both Urbanik touchdowns came in the first half as Penn State opened up a 20-0 gap.

His first score from one yard out capped a 56-yard drive following the opening kick. His second, again from a yard away, finished up a 69-yard drive in the second quarter. The highlight of the drive was Urbanik's 31-yard dash through the middle, as Penn State alternated from the I and T formations.

Toward the end of the first half, Dirk Nye climaxed a 59-yard drive with a five-yard sweep around left end that made it 20-0.

Second-string fullback Dave McNaughton scored Penn State's final touchdown in the fourth quarter on a spinning one-yard dive to end an 84-yard drive. Gary Wydman threw to Bill Huber for the two-point conversion, allowing for the 28-0 final.

If you're a trivia buff, Huber's two-point pass conversion was the *first* in the series since the introduction of the added PAT in 1958. Recall also that Penn State's Dave Hayes scored the first-ever two-point run conversion in the series in 1960. Also, to this point in the series, Pitt had failed to convert a two-point conversion against Penn State.

More trivia: With 11 seconds to play, Pitt got the ball on Penn State's 37-yard line. Ken Lucas managed to complete a 15-yard pass to Mike Rosborough, but his next throw was broken up, thus ending the game. Ken was the younger brother of quarterback Richie Lucas, who starred in the late '50s at Penn State.

Rip Engle had all of Sunday to contemplate the joys of his 28-0 victory over Michelosen's club. Said Rip, "Success lies not in never failing, but in rising every time you fail."

In his book, *Road to Number One*, author Ridge Riley says people were impressed with Rip's latest quip believing it was an original. But as Riley pointed out, Engle had stolen his favorite quote from that other grand football master, Woody Hayes.

The Lambert Trophy went to Penn State (6-4) even though Syracuse (7-3) would have been a better choice with victories over Pitt, Penn State, Army and UCLA.

Glenn Ressler became the first Lion center since Leon Gajecki (1940) to win All-America honors as well as Philadelphia's prestigious Maxwell Award. Zeke, as his teammates called him, had a fine career with the Baltimore Colts.

1965

Game 65

Lucas & Clark

Kenny Lucas wanted to enroll at Penn State. Badly. He had watched his older brother, Richie, carefully pick and choose the scholarship offers before finally deciding on Mt. Nittany. A place where Richie would be named to the All-American team in 1959. Yep, Richie Lucas had done all right for himself at Penn State. Even played two seasons with the Buffalo Bills. Kenny Lucas decided Penn State was where he wanted to go, too.

But Rip Engle didn't seem very intent on recruiting Kenny Lucas some four years after Richie had graduated. Anxious as Kenny was to letter at Penn State, Engle already had a sharp quarterback in Pete Liske and a fine back-up in Jack White. So, Kenny Lucas ended up at Pitt, where Coach John Michelosen made it known he appreciated the lad's many passing skills.

In what amounts to nothing short of poetic justice (or is it irony?), Kenny Lucas repaid Engle for the recruiting snub on Nov. 20, 1965 by leading Pitt to a bone-chilling 30-27 upset of the Lions before 35,567 at Pitt Stadium. Lucas ripped apart the Penn State secondary for 228 yards in the air (18 of 24) and masterminded a thrilling drive in the final 55 seconds that reached a crescendo on Frank Clark's winning 18-yard field goal with the score knotted at 27-27.

Though unlisted in the program as a kicker, Clark was nevertheless quite calm when he booted the final points with :03 showing on the clock. It was a gambling move by Michelosen, too, because had Clark missed, the Pitt coach would have been crucified for going with a kid whose previous "game" experience was two years on the bench. As it was, Clark's three points turned out to be the highlight of his collegiate career.

"I wasn't nervous," Clark said of the field goal. "I was more nervous when I tried the first field goal."

Clark missed a second-quarter field goal from 20 yards, partially because he came into the game with a bad back and was supposed to kick placements only.

Still, Clark's magical three-pointer would not have been possible without the poised leadership Kenny Lucas displayed on that frantic, final drive.

Starting at the Panther 40, Clark wheeled and dealed five straight passes to his shifty little halfback, Eric Crabtree. Penn State's coaching staff tried desperately to figure out how to stop the senior's sideline flares to Crabtree and Bob Longo. Longo's three catches, which brought the ball to the Lion 9-yard line, were made in heavy traffic. Lucas attempted to bootleg it from there but was pushed out of bounds at the 1. With three ticks remaining, Michelosen signaled for Clark.

What hurt Penn State more than Lucas or even Clark was Lion halfback Don Kunit, whose three early fumbles resulted in two Panther touchdowns. Kunit atoned for the sins with two fourth quarter touchdowns, but it wasn't enough.

Lucas zipped 13 passes into his receivers' arms as Pitt opened up a 20-0 bulge in the first half. The first score was a one-yard run by Dewey Chester. Then Longo caught a 41-yard TD pass over defensive back John Sladki, who got burned on the game's final drive, and finally fullback Barry McKnight smashed over from two yards out. That made it 20-0.

Penn State drove 52 yards at the start of the second half to cut the margin to 20-7. Fullback Dave McNaughton provided a large chunk of the yardage, and fumbled in midair while crossing the two-yard line. Luckily, the ball was snared by quarterback Jack White as he ran into the end zone.

McKnight's second score of the game gave Pitt a 27-7 lead as the third quarter ended. Kunit continued his slashing runs behind McNaughton's brutal blocking early in the last quarter as Penn State's 59-yard drive culminated with the latter's six-yard TD. Kunit's second touchdown later brought Penn State to within 27-21.

With less than four minutes remaining, Penn State began its final scoring drive of 54 yards as White found Kunit open three times for big gains all the way to the Pitt 6. On first down, White faked to McNaughton in the middle, and pitched to Kunit. The crafty senior slithered around end for a tying touchdown.

Tom Sherman had already kicked three extra points under pressure. There was no reason to suspect he'd miss the big one. But he did. It was Sherman's second miss in 20 attempts that season. Sherman would have finished wearing goat's horns, but Lucas and Clark saved him that embarrassment.

Although Penn State's Bob Riggle got the final kick with one second left in the game, his zig-zag run was for considerable yardage across the width of the field, but not enough straight ahead.

Pitt had ruined another Rip Engle season. Better yet, it had broken Penn State's national record of 26 straight winning seasons (the Lions ended up 5-5). Other than that, things were bad in Pittsburgh, where Coach John Michelosen watched his Panthers fall from a 9-1 mark in 1963 to successive losing seasons (3-5-2, 3-7). Michelosen got the ax shortly after as Dave Hart entered the picture.

During his 11-year tenure, Michelosen, a truly likable guy if you ever had the pleasure of knowing him, held Rip Engle to a 5-5-1 standoff. After his departure, which came amid controversy, Penn State proceeded to win 10 straight series games.

One last note regarding the Lucas legend. In 1958, Richie boomed a punt a series-record 53 yards during Penn State's 25-21 win over Pitt. On Nov. 20, 1965, that record gave way to the current one held by the Lions' Wayne Corbett (67 yards).

1966

Game 66

The Paterno Era Begins

The Coming of Paterno was deeply rooted. Rip Engle retired after the '65 season, saying he wanted to get out while the game was still fun and enjoy the little things he never had time for as a coach. Joe Paterno had been made an assistant coach that season as part of the formality of assuring a smooth changeover once Rip stepped down. Were it not for Rip's liking Paterno back in 1950, none of this would have happened. Rip, then the head coach at Brown, was impressed with Paterno's ability. In the words of the late Stanley Woodward, "He (Paterno) can't run and he can't pass. All he can do is think and win."

Joe quarterbacked two Engle teams to 7-2 and 8-1 records at Brown. In June of 1950, while Paterno was working with Rip's quarterbacks, Engle posed this question to him: Would you like to come to State College with me after you graduate rather than attend law school? Legend has it, Engle offered the spot to one of his other assistants, but was turned down. Paterno knew he had a rendezvous with destiny. He accepted Engle's offer to coach the offensive backs. Thus began Joe Paterno's association with Penn State football.

It's doubtful whether Paterno will ever forget his first meeting as a coach against Pitt. After all, how can you possibly forget slaughtering your opponent 48-24 in what is undoubtedly Eastern football's most bitter annual clash?

New Penn State Head Coach Joe Paterno gives instructions to his quarterback, Tom Sherman.

Penn State Jars Pitt in Finale As Campbell Scores 3 TDs

Rookie Coach Dave Hart was simply devastated afterward. "We can't run," Hart lamented. "I saw it was a long afternoon. I'm glad it's over. It could have been 48-0."

Hart said the only positive thing about the game was Pitt's next season would be starting the following day. Unbeknownst to Dave Hart, all three seasons he coached at Pitt would end the same way—with 1-9 records.

Penn State decided quite early to put this game on ice. The Lions sprang ahead 27-0 in the first half as quarterback Tom Sherman threw two touchdown passes, one to tight end Ted Kwalick, the other to the opposite end, Jack Curry. This tended to silence the 30,000-plus at Pitt Stadium.

When it was all over, Sherman had completed 10 of 16 passes for 146 yards and three touchdowns; wingback Bobby Campbell had shredded Pitt's line for 137 yards and three scores, and Penn State had rolled up an amazing 546 yards (total offense). That sum is *believed* to be a series record, but because there are gaps in statistical records prior to 1940, no one knows for sure. Whatever, two years later that record fell.

Hart told reporters he never thought a team like Penn State, which was of 5-5 caliber for the second straight season, could score 48 points on him. To which *Philadelphia Inquirer* reporter Charlie Frush echoed his famous rejoinder, "It was easy."

Tailback Mike Irwin pitter-pattered 34 yards with a punt to set up Sherman's three-yard touchdown pass to Kwalick in the opening minutes. Irwin dashed 22 yards with another first-quarter punt, paving the way for Campbell's 16-yard touchdown off a reverse. That made it 13-0.

A six-yard pitchout to Irwin in the second quarter upped the score to 19-0. Pitt quarterback Ed James threw an interception which led to the Lions' next touchdown. This time Sherman hurled deep to Curry for a 30-yarder that left the Pitt defenders choking on their own dust. Irwin's two-point run conversion gave the Lions a fat 27-0 bulge.

"Nobody had made much going inside against Pitt, not even Notre Dame, Syracuse and Miami," Paterno remarked. "So we knew we had to get Campbell and Irwin running outside more."

On Penn State's first drive of the second half, Campbell took a pitchout at the Pitt 41, then outran the secondary for a 33-0 lead. That plus Irwin's 21-yard kickoff return consumed all of 18 seconds. Poor Dave Hart. It really was going to be a long afternoon for his Panthers.

Panther quarterback Ed James hurled three touchdown passes in the final 30 minutes as Pitt attempted to claw its way back. Actually, James played a fairly good game, completing 21 of 46 passes for 203 yards. His favorite target was tight end Bob Longo. He retrieved seven passes for 146 yards, broke Pitt's single-season reception record with his 48th catch, and set another single-season mark with 732 yards via receptions. Longo graduated in 1967 as the school's all-time receiving leader with 1,621 yards. Gordon Jones would break that mark a decade later, but Long is still No. 2 on the charts today.

Getting back to James, he threw TD passes of five yards to Joe Jones, six to Longo and 32 to Gerald Rife. Running back James Flanigan scored on a nine-yard run accounting for Pitt's final touchdown.

Paterno raised the ire of Hart, among others, when his punter, Wayne Corbett, caught Pitt napping on a fourth-and-five and fired an embarrassing 32-yard completion to Curry. With the ball at the Pitt 11, reserve quarterback Jack White threw a TD pass to Bob Vukmar, making it 48-12.

Paterno was accused of running up the score. Joe told his detractors his club would play "every game" as if it were behind. That answer seemed to place Paterno's football guidelines in the proper perspective by which future generations of writers could measure him.

1967

Game 67

The Records of Sherman and Curry

After Pete Liske graduated, the quarterback slot on Mt. Nittany became an open field. The entries were many, but one man, sophomore Jack White, seemed the heir apparent in 1964. He alternated with Gary Wydman that season, then alternated with Tom Sherman in 1965, before getting the tentative nod in 1966. White was pushed hard by Tom Sherman, who was a year behind him. By the middle of the '66 season, Sherman had overtaken White.

Pitt Coach Dave Hart remarked in 1966 that he was impressed with Sherman. He was undoubtedly influenced by the young man's three touchdown passes that day. After Penn State completed another routine decapitation of Pitt, 42-6, on Nov. 25, 1967 at Beaver Stadium, Hart declared that Sherman was one of the "most underrated quarterbacks in the country." By no means was this a rash statement on Hart's part for he had been a witness, along with 34,042 others, to Sherman's school record four touchdown passes, a record that still stands today.

Tight end Jack Curry, who wasn't blessed with the clips or recognition of the guy who lined up less frequently than he (Ted Kwalick), finished his three-year career that afternoon with 16, count 'em, 16 Penn State records. Incredible as it may sound, Jack Curry never played pro ball. Too small, scouts said.

Jack Curry, Penn State tight end, held 16 school records when he graduated.

Penn State Rolls as Sherman Riddles Pitt

Let's dispense with the records first. We'll start with Mr. Sherman's seven school records:

–Touchdown passes one game, 4.
–Touchdown passes one season, 12.
–Pass completions one season, 104.
–Yards passing one season, 1,616.
–Total offense one season, 1,761.
–Career passing yardage, 2,588.
–Career total offense, 2,850.

As for Mr. Curry:

–Receptions one season, 42.
–Career receptions, 117
–Receptions one season by a senior, 41.
         by a junior, 34.
         by a sophomore, 42.
–Receptions one game, 10.
–Receptions one game by a senior, 9.
         by a sophomore, 10.
–Career receiving yardage, 1,837.
–Receiving yardage one season, 681.
–Receiving yardage one season by a senior, 681.
         by a junior, 584.
         by a sophomore, 572.
–Receiving yardage, one game, 148.
–Receiving yardage by a senior, 104.
         by a sophomore, 148.

Fifteen records established by Jack Curry between 1965-67 still stand today! No other Penn State athlete has ever dominated a single category as decisively as Jack Curry. Believe it or not, Kwalick, not Curry, made All-American in 1967.

As for the game, Penn State ran a string of 14s on the scoreboard through the first three quarters. Pitt also had a string of numbers right under the 14s—all zeroes—until the last quarter.

In the first quarter, Sherman hit Don Abbey with a five-yard scoring pass and offensive tackle Rich Buzin later recovered Abbey's end zone fumble for another score giving Penn State a 14-0 lead. In the second quarter, Curry, who finished the game with seven catches and 103 yards, took a 16-yard Sherman pass in for a touchdown. Then Charlie Pittman, a newcomer on Mt. Nittany, skirted around end for a two-yard score which made it 28-0.

Fullback Dan Lucyk scored on a five-yard pass from Sherman in the third quarter and Abbey got his second TD pass of the day, this one 23 yards, which gave Penn State an embarrassing 42-0 lead.

Pitt's only score came in the fourth quarter after many of Paterno's regulars were on the bench. Quarterback Frankie Gustine, who would later open a popular bar/restaurant not far from Pitt Stadium in Oakland, lofted a three-yard pass to George (Doc) Medich but the pass conversion failed. Medich later pitched for the Pirates.

Paterno took offense when someone suggested that Sherman's 16 of 24 for 209 yards passing was achieved against a Kleenex pass defense. "When Sherman is on, he's a very much underrated quarterback," Joe said, echoing what Hart was saying in the other locker room.

"It was a great season and certainly a great game today. Pitt's our big game and I was real proud of the fact they (Lions) kept first things first and didn't get wrapped up in this bowl business."

Bowl business meant the Gator, where the Lions would blow a 17-0 halftime lead against Florida State and return north with a tie.

One of the truly classic lines ever to come out of a losing dressing room was uttered during the Pitt-Penn State meeting in 1967. Dave Hart knew Penn State was good. The Lions were only a tie away from an 8-2-1 season. Somehow, Hart never imagined Penn State was *that* good. Or 36 points better than 1-9 Pitt.

"Penn State offensively is stronger than I anticipated," said the poker-faced Hart. "This might have been their peak game."

1968

Game 68

The Humiliation Continues

It's not easy being upstaged by a beauty contest. Especially by a beauty queen. That, however, is exactly what happened in Pitt Stadium on Nov. 23, 1968 when Penn State again annihilated Pitt, 65-9 (ouch!).

One of Pittsburgh's finest had been selected the ECAC Queen from among representative schools Penn State, Syracuse, Buffalo, Boston College, Penn and Villanova. When Mary Ann Zovko's name blared across the public address system, the throng of 31,224 cheered lustily. Naturally, this was a most uncomfortable position for Pitt's players to be in. On the other hand, you could look at the brighter side. At least Miss Zovko had given Pitt fans something to cheer about, which is more than you can say about Dave Hart's 1-9 Panthers.

Hart was beside himself by now. For three years, all he heard and read in the newspapers was how he had kicked Joe Paterno's butt in the spring recruiting wars. The evidence was usually found in the final score of the freshman games. Pitt always won. (The Lion freshmen coach at the time was Earl Bruce, now head coach at Ohio State).

Hart was fired after the 1968 season but even his detractors admit that while he failed to get maximum performance out of his recruits,

Charlie Pittman, Penn State halfback, tied Lenny Moore's single season
scoring record, 1968.

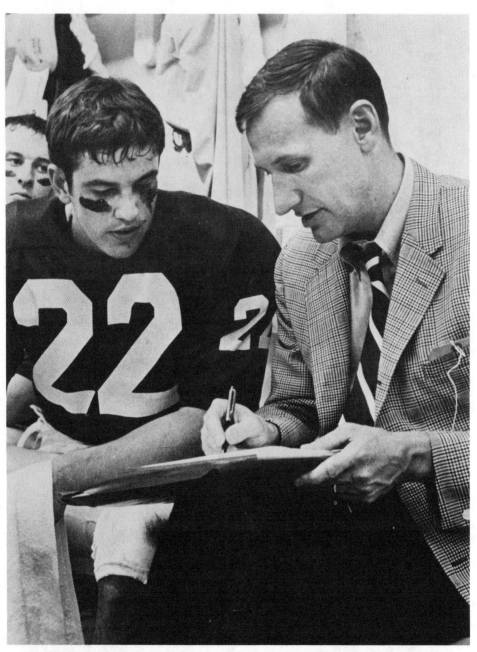

Chuck Burkhart, Penn State halfback, listens to backfield coach, George Welsh, 1968.

he was nonetheless a great salesman when it came to Pitt football.

For the second straight week Penn State scored over 50 points, a feat that rested uneasily upon Joe Paterno's shoulders. Paterno, attempting to keep the score down, pulled starting quarterback Chuck Burkhart in the second half and replaced him with Mike Cooper. Cooper immediately rose to the occasion and hurled a 19-yard scoring pass to Tim Horst. The touchdown gave Penn State a 58-9 lead. When Cooper went to the bench, the gleam of accomplishment still fresh in his eyes, Paterno scolded him.

"I didn't want to throw in the second half," Paterno explained. "But Cooper was calling the plays. Like I said last week (after beating Maryland, 57-13), I don't enjoy a situation like this."

Even though some of his Lions did. It was a very productive day from a stat standpoint. Kicker Bob Garthwaite nailed a 23-yard field goal and seven extra points. Junior Charlie Pittman scored three touchdowns in a 35-point second quarter, tying Lenny Moore's single-season record of 13 touchdowns. Bobby Campbell picked up 104 yards rushing and Burkhart completed seven of 10 passes for 143 more. Included among all those yards was Burkhart's 63-yard TD pass to Ted Kwalick, who had five receptions for 121 yards.

Naturally, in a game of such scoring magnitude there were a number of records established. Linebacker Dennis Onkotz ran back a Panther punt 63 yards (no touchdown). His 71-yard return the following season is the longest ever against Pittsburgh by a Penn State player.

The significant records in this game, oddly enough, belonged to Pitt, the team that lost by 56 points while scoring a piddly nine. The Panthers set four series records.

Panther quarterback Dave Havern threw 54 passes, completing 29 for 314 yards. That's three records right there. Split end Harry Orszulak caught a record 16 passes for 158 yards. As of 1981, all four continue to stand as both series and Pitt individual records.

Writers attending the 1968 game named Orszulak the game's most outstanding player. Hart explained later his game plan was for Havern to throw as much as possible.

"We had to throw those quick outs," Hart said. "Penn State has such a great rush that it's tough getting time to throw deep. So we went to the quick outs and hoped Orszulak could break a few plays with his speed."

Havern spent a frantic afternoon fleeing for his life on more than one of those pass completions. The men chasing him were none other than defensive tackles Mike Reid and Steve Smear. One of the more comical Panther miscues involved Havern. After Reid and

Smear decked him, he fumbled. The ball bounced off the trailing official and kept rolling toward the Pitt goal line. Reid pounced on it at the Panther 4-yard line for a 35-yard Havern loss. It was that kind of game.

Penn State wrapped up the season beating Syracuse, then pulled out that amazing Orange Bowl victory, 15-14, over Kansas to finish 11-0 and second in both wire polls.

It should be pointed out that Paterno was more tolerant of his players calling plays and even changing them back in 1968 than he is today. Recall Paterno admitted Cooper deliberately disobeyed his orders not to throw the ball in the second half against Pitt.

In the Orange Bowl victory, Burkhart's fabulous completion to Campbell that got the ball to the Kansas 3-yard line was the result of both agreeing to ignore Paterno's play, which was to fake the Jayhawks out by throwing the ball out of the end zone, thereby giving the impression Penn State was desperate.

Burkhart again ignored Paterno by going over from the 3-yard line to cut Penn State's deficit to 14-13. Paterno had insisted that Pittman take the ball. Of course, Campbell's two-point run conversion, which gave the Lions their victory, was Paterno's doing. What does this all have to do with Pitt-Penn State? Simply this: Paterno had an extraordinary group of athletes whose self-confidence was immeasurable. They felt they were in better command of the game than he was at times. Paterno's lenience in allowing his troops to have their own way in the Pitt game was a sign these kids were hard to place a lid over.

In time, Paterno would become a stricter disciplinarian. He—and only he—would be calling the plays.

1969

Game 69

Onkotz Loses a Shoe; Lions Lose a Championship

Dennis Onkotz had established quite a reputation as a shifty linebacker with an acute sense of awareness whenever the ball was in the air by the time 1969 rolled around. Onkotz left Penn State the proud holder of four interception records. But Denny had another flair for the sensational. He liked to run back punts.

Against Pitt in 1968, he ran one back a series record 63 yards to the Panther 2. Dennis was unhappy because he hadn't scored. A week earlier he returned a punt 41 yards against Maryland only to be chopped down at the 1. It was frustrating. He wondered if he'd ever cross that goal line.

On Nov. 22, 1969, Dennis Onkotz broke his 1968 series record by galloping 71 yards (41 of which were traversed without a shoe) against the Panthers. Again, Denny had failed in his attempt to cross that coveted goal line, as Pitt's Dennis Ferris pulled him down at the 5.

Onkotz' punt return was a turning point in the game. With the score tied at 7-7 late in the third quarter, and with the ball deep inside Pitt territory, Charlie Pittman carved out the Lions' go-ahead touch-

Dennis Onkotz, Penn State All-American linebacker, 1969.

down on a four-yard run. Following Mike Reitz' extra point, Penn State led 14-7. Onkotz finished the game with eight tackles, one interception and was voted the James Coogan Award as MVP.

As the game moved into the fourth quarter, Panther first-year coach Carl DePasqua made a rational judgment that ultimately cost him the game. With the ball on the Lions' 32-yard line, DePasqua elected to punt on fourth down and seven but Joe Spicko's kick went straight up in the air, then landed in approximately the same place.

"Why did I do it?" DePasqua answered. "Intuition. A certain feeling. I hoped we could keep them down there. There's always a possibility of a fumble."

Sophomore fullback Franco Harris bulled 41 yards shortly after—on one shoe, no less—to the Pitt 31. Quarterback Chuck Burkhart moved the Lions inside the 20, then Pittman broke three tackles to score on a 17-yard run. Penn State led 21-7. The game was over for all intents and purposes.

A Paul Johnson interception gave the Lions a first down at the Panther 33 later that period. That set up Don Abbey's 18-yard score that accounted for the 27-7 final. Although much improved over the year before, the Panther offense was held without a first down in the second half, a half which always seemed to bring out the best in Joe Paterno's boys that season.

Harris' 24-yard run in the first quarter had given Penn State a 7-0 edge but Pitt tied the game in the second quarter after a roughing-the-kicker penalty against George Landis added new hope to a Panther drive at the Penn State 37. Panther back Tony Esposito clicked off six yards for a touchdown and Spicko's PAT made it 7-7.

In addition to Onkotz' punt return record, Lion safety Neal Smith set a new single-season interception standard with nine. That record would become 10 a week later against North Carolina. Smith and Pete Harris (1978) share the record today.

Most people remember 1969 because of the incredible brouhaha over Number One. Penn State (11-0), which stretched its unbeaten streak to 28 games against Pitt, went on to defeat Missouri in the Orange Bowl, 10-3. The 30-game unbeaten streak was the longest in college football. Penn State elected to face Missouri in the Orange Bowl rather than hold out for a possible match against Texas in the Cotton Bowl.

"If we can beat North Carolina and Missouri, we still have a chance (for Number One)," Paterno had said following the Pitt game.

But when No. 1 Ohio State was upset, suddenly Texas jumped in

Joe Paterno in action prior to a game.

front and was being touted for No. 1 honors.

Probably no one in the state of Pennsylvania will ever forget President Nixon "awarding" Texas No. 1 on national television after the Longhorns' 21-17 win over Notre Dame.

Paterno was outraged. "I've got to stick up for my kids," he fumed. "I put a lot of pressure on them when I said they were No. 1. I can't sit back and let Richard Nixon say someone else is No. 1. I'd be a lousy coach if I did."

When the President awarded Penn State a Presidential plaque for holding the nation's longest unbeaten streak, Paterno's statement was succint.

". . . it would seem to me to be a waste of his very valuable time to present Penn State with a plaque for something it already undisputedly owns—the nation's longest winning and unbeaten records."

So much for Richard Milhous Nixon.

1970

Game 70

Beat Pitt, Challenge Dartmouth

Joe Paterno made it five in a row over Pitt with an easy 35-15 victory at Beaver Stadium, the first time in three seasons the Lions had hosted their traditional rival. Fullback Franco Harris, now a junior, scored three touchdowns and ran for 93 yards. Classmate Lydell Mitchell led all ball-carriers with 110 yards.

Pitt managed only three first downs in the opening 30 minutes, then was held to minus-eight yards and no first downs in the third quarter. Although Paterno insisted his club didn't do anything special to prepare for Pitt, Panther Coach Carl DePasqua was shell-shocked. When asked for his comments after the game, DePasqua refused. A Pitt assistant uttered the now-famous post-game quote, "Call back in January."

Penn State raced out to a 35-9 lead in that memorable first half. Joel Ramich, whose name you won't run across very much in this series, trotted 25 yards for the Lions' first touchdown. Harris then broke into the open field for a 39-yard sprint which made it 14-0.

A Penn State fumble gave Pitt its first points, on a 29-yard Joe Spicko field goal. But the Lions weren't ready to call it quits just yet. Harris capped off a 71-yard drive in the second quarter with a one-yard plunge to make it 21-3. On State's next possession, sophomore quarterback John Hufnagel completed a 55-yard strike to tight end

Jim McCord giving Penn State a first down at the Panther 3-yard line. Fran Ganter took it from there. Now it was 28-3.

A mix-up in Penn State's coverage which saw too many Lions defending the wrong side of a screen pass, helped Pitt quarterback Dave Havern complete a 62-yarder to Dennis Ferris. Ferris got to the Lion 3 before Tony Esposito scored. Ferris also scored Pitt's fourth quarter touchdown.

Although most teams might have been satisfied with a 28-9 lead, the Lions were still honing their claws. Beating up on the Panthers had become a fond tradition since Paterno took over and the boys enjoyed it.

Mitchell, one of the most exciting backs to play at Penn State, broke free for a 40-yard gain in the final minute of the second quarter, added 10 more to the Pitt 1-yard line, then allowed Harris to do the scoring honors. Voila! 35-9.

In just 30 minutes, the Lions' offensive juggernaut churned out 242 yards on the ground and 315 overall, while limiting Pitt to a mere nine plays. No wonder DePasqua felt ashamed to meet the press.

What the members of the Eastern elite wanted to find out was why DePasqua told Havern and back-up John Hogan to keep the ball on the ground when Pitt was behind by 26 points. Havern threw only three passes all day, Hogan 12.

So while Pitt was trying to ram it down Penn State's throat in the second half—which didn't work—Paterno was throwing in his reserves (including second-and-third-string quarterbacks Mike Cooper and Bob Parsons).

"I thought we were going to have to throw more against them," Paterno said. "We were too cautious in the second half. I was afraid we couldn't move them. Notre Dame couldn't move them until they threw."

The Irish might have struggled running against Pitt two weeks earlier, but you'd never guess by looking at the 46-13 final.

Pitt defensive tackle Lloyd Weston said Paterno's 7-3 club was "as good as any team." When asked how he arrived at that assessment, Weston replied, "They hit quicker and lower." Lower, eh?

The Penn State players rejected bids from the Peach and Liberty Bowls following the game. Playing in three straight bowls didn't seem to have much bearing on the decision.

"We finished 7-3 and we're willing to live through history with that record," said linebacker Jack Ham, an All-American that season.

No, the Lions didn't want to go to a bowl but they did want to shut the mouths of the people at Dartmouth, the leading Lambert Trophy candidate with a 9-0 record.

Mitchell broke Tom Sherman's 1965-67 record for total offense yardage by gaining 181 on 21 carries for a career log of 2,851. He broke it by a single yard. Some years later, a fellow named Chuck Fusina would exceed Mitchell's mark with some 2,300 yards to spare.

Mitchell also scored a game-high three touchdowns against Pitt and along with Harris (61 yards), reserve fullback Tom Donchez (45) and Hufnagel (5), helped Penn State pad its rushing figures to 350 for the game. Huffy completed 7 of 11 tosses for an additional 168 yards as the Lions used their Texas Instruments to calculate 530 total yards in the game. Not bad for a team that seemed disenchanted afterward because it sensed there was no way it would collar a national championship, no matter who it played in a bowl game. After all, beating the hell out of Big 8 and Southwest Conference bowl teams had become a norm at Penn State. So had taking a back seat to someone else when it came to award No. 1.

So, the Lions went out and dissected Pitt with all the fervor of a South Philadelphia butcher.

Among the highlights of the meat festival was Hufnagel's 52-yard bomb to Bob Parsons for a touchdown plus his 49-yard scoring pass to Chuck Herd. It was 48-0 midway into the third quarter when reserve quarterback Steve Joachim made an appearance. The highly-recruited sophomore zipped a 13-yard pass to Gary Debes for Penn State's final touchdown of the day. Joachim, unhappy about limited playing time on Mt. Nittany, transferred after the season. He started for Temple in 1973-74.

After the Pitt game, the Lions had to settle back while Nebraska, Oklahoma, Auburn and Alabama sifted through the bowl bids. Penn State got sloppy fifths, which explains how its players spent Jan. 1 in the Cotton Bowl humbling almighty Texas, the previous year's national champion, 30-6.

Not everyone was thrilled at waiting so long for the bowl bid. Sitting in the dressing room after the Pitt game, linebacker Charlie Zapiec, who would be voted to the All-America team that season, told a reporter, "We're the last rated team to get a bowl bid. It makes you kind of mad to know that people think so low of you.

"I feel like I've played on two national championship teams—no matter what anybody says. What else are we supposed to do?"

The critics answered Zapiec by suggesting Penn State strengthen its schedule. Translation: dump Iowa, Army and Air Force and replace them with southwest teams or Big 8 schools. They also pointed to a 31-11 loss to Tennessee after the Pitt game as one reason why the Lions couldn't be taken seriously.

Penn St. Rips Pitt, Challenges Dartmouth

In a move he later regretted, Paterno popped off and challenged Dartmouth to meet Penn State at Shea Stadium or any place of its choosing to decide who should represent the East. It was foolish on Paterno's part to suggest that a school of Penn State's size (budget, scholarships etc.) take on a lowly Ivy school like Dartmouth. Paterno figured since the Ivies were screaming for Lambert Trophy recognition, well, if you're going to feast with the reigning Beast of the East, you'd better be prepared to do the dishes.

Dartmouth Athletic Director Seaver Peters was incensed with Paterno's suggestion because Joe was fully aware the Ivies permitted only nine games — not 10. The Big Green's coach, Bob Blackman, accused Paterno of "grandstanding." The furor was made worse when the New York press, naturally, goaded Dartmouth with suggestions that such a game could be called the Lambert Bowl.

Years later, Paterno said he was only half-serious at his suggestion but in retrospect, it can be stated with some measure of accuracy that Joe was *very* serious. At least he accomplished one thing, however. The Ivies learned to pick on schools their own size.

The entire complexion of the series changed between 1960 and 1970. During that period, Penn State won eight games and bombarded Pitt for 356 points. In winning two games and scoring just 139 points, Pitt now found itself trailing Penn State in overall point production (877-959) but still clung to a slim lead in the series, 35-32-3. It wouldn't be much longer before Penn State gained an upper hand entirely in the series.

1971

Game 71

More Broken Records

After several years of good-to-excellent weather, a blustery, wet day greeted the 71st meeting between Pitt and Penn State in Pittsburgh. Less than 40,000 showed up, no doubt the result of Pitt's abominable 3-7 record. Penn State came into the game ranked in the Top 10 at 9-0. You didn't need a lineup card to figure out who Lydell Mitchell, Franco Harris and John Hufnagel were by now. The 'Burghers still had nightmares from past games in which those three pretty much had their way with Pitt.

Panther Coach Carl DePasqua threw in the towel before the game ever got underway by electing to kick off after winning the toss. If ever a leader sent a battle cry to the enemy that his troops were expecting the worse, DePasqua's choice to kick was such.

Penn State held a modest 7-0 lead after one quarter on Mitchell's 16-yard run, then blew the game open with a 28-point outburst in the second period. Oh yes, the final score was, ahem, 55-18. If you're the sadistic type who's been keeping a macabre accounting of the past five series meetings, then you already know Penn State was averaging 45 points a game (including 1971) while holding Pitt to 11. That should give you an idea of how mismatched the series had become heading into the '70s.

Only two records fell in this game. Italian kicker Alberto Vitiello nailed seven of his eight extra-point attempts for a school record 59. His single-season mark has yet to be duplicated.

233

Alberto Vitiello, Penn State kicker, converted seven PATs in the 1971 game.

John Hufnagel, Penn State quarterback and Coach Joe Paterno.

Penn State suffered through jokes about Eastern football and
'What's a Nittany Lion?' the week prior to the Cotton Bowl game.
Joe Paterno's gang got its licks in on the field and that's all anyone
really cared about, anyway.

1972

Game 72

Huffy Blows the
Panthers Down

If America's self-proclaimed "gonzo journalist,", Dr. Hunter S. Thompson, had been covering these games in the '70s, he would have undoubtedly written a book titled "Fear and Loathing on Mt. Nittany," where Penn State was terrorizing its visitors.

By 1972, the Pitt football program had sunk to the very depths of mediocrity. DePasqua was coaching what would be his final season in Oakland. The once proud Panthers, who used to turn out eight-and nine-win seasons like so many new kewpie dolls, now struggled just to win three and four games. Pitt won only once in 11 tries during DePasqua's final season. His overall record was 13-29.

Games such as these tend to bring out the best (and worst) in sportswriters. Because there is so much scoring and so little competition, the guys in the press box try to be cute. Sometimes they pull it off.

Philadelphia Inquirer reporter John Flynn labeled Penn State's 49-27 rout over Pitt a "Bummerroski." Flynn's best line, however, was analyzing the correct time and place when the game got out of hand in Beaver Stadium.

"The turning point of this game," Flynn wrote, "was the day John Hufnagel was born."

Hufnagel's final bid for the Heisman Trophy that year was indeed impressive. Huffy completed 12 of 20 passes for 260 yards and three touchdowns. He graduated that spring with 16 records to his name, seven of which still stand as of 1981.

In sealing DePasqua's fate, Hufnagel fired a 31-yard scoring pass to Jimmy Scott, a 21-yarder to Dave Bland and a 41-yarder to Chuck Herd. Joe Paterno pulled him for sophomore Tom Shuman with less

John Hufnagel, Penn State quarterback.

than nine minutes remaining in the third quarter because, as Joe said, "I thought about the other guy (DePasqua) and didn't want to run it up." Penn State had already run up 35 unanswered points on the board, including a 59-yard punt return TD by Gary Hayman which followed an 11-yard scoring run by Bob Nagle.

Air Nittany's 329 yards were a series record. As in past routs, Pitt also managed to establish a series record, though it couldn't match Penn State for total points. John Hogan, the Panthers' senior quarterback from Charleroi, Pa., replaced sophomore starter Billy Daniels in the fourth quarter. Hogan turned in the best all-time, one-quarter performance by a quarterback, zipping four touchdown passes, two of which were cradled by Bill Englert, the others by Stan Ostrowski and Todd Toerper, the latter being the longest score (33 yards).

Only two other quarterbacks, Vanderbilt's Boyce Smith (1957) and Temple's Terry Gregory (1976) have thrown four touchdown passes against a Lion defense. True, four TD passes in a game are not all that spectacular. But four in one quarter are something special. That's one scoring pass every four minutes.

Paterno kept the rushing stats down in this one to 129 by pulling halfback John Cappelletti (77 yards, 11 carries) after two quarters. The *Inquirer's* Mr. Flynn said that Joe's actions were worthy of "Humanitarian of the Year."

The victory enabled Penn State to finish the regular season with a 10-1 record. In 28 games Hufnagel had played, Penn State won 26. More credence that the young man might win the Heisman.

"I'd give anything to win the Heisman," Huffy said. "But I don't know any more about my chances than what I read. However, I consider myself a candidate and all candidates have a chance— even George McGovern."

Hufnagel's droll humor was a signal to the press that he really didn't expect to win the Heisman just like no one really expected McGovern to oust Richard Nixon from the White House. Huffy was selected to the All-America team with teammates Bruce Bannon (DE) and John Skourpan (LB).

Penn State lost 14-0 in the Sugar Bowl to Oklahoma, the first time a Lion team had been shut out in post-season play.

DePasqua was fired as Pitt promised "A Major Change in Pitt Football." It came in the person of Johnny Majors, who was lured away from Iowa State at a considerable salary. Pitt's program resuscitated almost immediately as Majors led the Panthers to a 6-4-1 record in 1973 and their first bowl appearance in 17 seasons.

1973

Game 73

Cappy

Besides canning Pitt alum Carl DePasqua and importing Johnny Majors from the Midwest, Pitt also decided to drop out of the "Big Four Agreement," which was Eastern football's equivalent of NATO. The pact was nothing more than a verbal commitment from Penn State, Pitt, West Virginia and Syracuse to abide by a list of standards pertaining to recruiting, admissions, grants-in-aid and red-shirting.

Although no one was saying it "officially," you got the impression Johnny Majors wasn't attempting to rescue any program that limited him in scholarship offers and the red-shirting of injured athletes. Syracuse Coach Ben Schwartzwalder, who had a long and famed rivalry with Rip Engle, retired that season, but not before getting his digs in on Penn State, claiming the Lions were cheating on the agreement.

The 1973 Pitt-Penn State affair was the only one that paired Lion tailback John Cappelletti against Pitt's freshman sensation, Tony Dorsett. Although both scored a touchdown, the game offered no contest as Cappy, the James Coogan Award winner, clearly out-fueled his foe, 161-77 in yards.

And Penn State clearly outplayed Pitt in the second half, rallying from a 13-3 deficit to win in easy fashion, 35-13. The victory knotted the series at 35 wins apiece with three ties. Recall that Pitt once held a 30-19 advantage on Penn State back in 1951.

John Cappelletti, Penn State Heisman Trophy winner, 1973.

Johnny Majors, Pitt Head Coach, 1973 to 1976.

Cappy rushed 37 times to Dorsett's 20 and finished his senior year with 1,522 yards in 286 carries and 17 touchdowns. Dorsett, the greatest freshman runner in the game at the time, achieved 1,586 yards in 288 tries and 12 touchdowns. Dorsett was also the first Panther to break the 1,000-yard mark in a single season.

Panther Coach Johnny Majors summed up Cappy's running as follows: "He just kept coming at us and coming at us," Majors said. "He got a lot of help from the fullbacks and Penn State's offensive line reminds me a lot of those great Nebraska teams; but Cappelletti gets a lot of it with his second effort."

Dorsett's 14-yard run and Carson Long's 31-yard field goal provided Pitt with its 13 first-half points. Chris Bahr's 40-yarder accounted for Penn State's. (Long also had a 50-yard boomer in this game.)

Lion Coach Joe Paterno said he didn't make an oratory address at the half.

"I didn't have to," Paterno said. "These boys have got an awful lot of pride. Listen, you gotta remember the seniors on this team have lost only three games and never lost in Beaver Stadium."

And while Cappy and Penn State erupted for 32 second-half points, the defense smothered Pitt. Particularly effective that afternoon at University Park, Pa., were linebackers Tom Hull and Chris Devlin. They shut off Pitt's option attack, and threw Dorsett for some big losses. Devlin also intercepted a Billy Daniel's pass to set up a Bahr field goal. Daniels was sacked three times in the final 30 minutes.

"The best defense I've faced all year," Dorsett commented. "They hit me a little harder than Notre Dame and they pursued quicker. They are really goooood."

Bob Nagle's one-yard run in the third quarter, plus Gary Hayman's two-point conversion off a Tom Shuman pass, brought Penn State to within 13-11. Pitt put up a valiant goal line stand which seemed to leave it empty after the score.

A minute into the final quarter Cappelletti scored on a five-yard run. Then Hull intercepted Daniel, running 27 yards for another touchdown. Shuman fired a 32-yard scoring pass to Chuck Herd, and Bahr blasted home a 45-yard field goal. In less than 10 minutes Penn State cranked out 24 points to turn defeat into victory.

"Boy," said a winded Majors, "they had their backs to the wall and then they came out supercharged and just took it to us.

"Their defense kept the pressure on us and their offense kept battering and butting. They controlled the ball and never gave us any room to run. They're bigger and boy, they're physical; they just

John Cappelletti, and Coach Joe Paterno at the Heisman Trophy banquet in New York, 1973.

"The Heisman Pose", 1973.

wore us down."

Cappelletti's performance enabled him to clinch the Heisman Trophy that season, the first in school history. His speech at the Downtown Athletic Club in New York City that December was—and still is—the proudest moment in the award's history. John dedicated the award to his younger brother, Joey, who later died of leukemia.

"I thought about it since the Heisman was announced 10 days ago," John said at the end of the address. "This is to dedicate a trophy that a lot of people earned . . .

"The youngest member of my family, Joseph, is very ill. He has leukemia. If I can dedicate this trophy to him tonight and give him a couple of days of happiness, this is worth everything. I think a lot of people think that I go through a lot on Saturdays and during the week as most athletes do, and you get your bumps and bruises and it is a terrific battle out there on the field.

"Only for me, it is on Saturdays and it's only in the fall. For Joseph, it is all year 'round and it is a battle that is unending with him and he puts up with much more than I'll ever put up with and I think that this trophy is more his than mine because he has been a great inspiration to me."

Penn State defeated Charley McClendon and LSU in the Orange Bowl, 14-9. The Lions' 12-0 record was the best in the country. Paterno conducted his famous "Paterno Poll" and said his club voted unanimously to rank itself No. 1, even though the wire services saw fit to rank Penn State fifth. Cappelletti, Randy Crowder (DT), and Ed O'Neil (LB) made the All-America team; 10 Lions were later drafted by the NFL.

Pitt, led by Dorsett's heroics, went to the Fiesta Bowl and lost 28-7 to Arizona State. Tony, however, was able to cherish his own special moment—he was the only Panther selected to the All-America squad.

1974

Game 74

Bahr Steals Dorsett's Show

Never one to allow money to stand in the way of sports coverage, Penn State's student-run newspaper, *The Daily Collegian*, decided to spend a few extra bucks in 1974 and scout the Lions' opposition on the road. That fall, *Collegian* Sports Editor Rick Starr and his two assistants traveled to Pittsburgh to watch the Pitt-USC game, to find out who this kid Tony Dorsett really was and why people couldn't seem to utter intelligible sentences about him without slurring words in the rush of excitement.

In order to fully prep his readers for the barrage of Dorsett coverage the following Monday, Starr had *Collegian* cartoonist Tom Gibb draw one of his many hilarious caricatures depicting three wayward writers traveling by a dog-drawn cart to Pittsburgh. The cartoon ran as a house ad for most of the week. Starr figured he could justify the expenses on this trip if all 30,000 *Collegians* sold out (they were free) on campus.

Gibb's cartoon was a hit among staffers and as usual, the phone calls came into the newspaper's office complimenting Gibb's outrageous sense of humor. Gibb's cartoon made the *Collegian's* football writers look foolish. Students loved it when Gibb made people look foolish. He did it to University President John Oswald just about every day.

246

They're off and writing, but in different directions this time as the Daily Collegian Sports initiates a new policy, bringing our readers live coverage of the top college football action across the country all season long. For the upcoming weekend Tim Panaccio heads for Pittsburgh where he'll be on hand at Pitt Stadium for Saturday's Pitt-USC game. Rick Starr will be heading westward for South Bend, Indiana, and a look at Notre Dame's first home pep rally Friday night. Then he'll continue on to Iowa City Saturday where the Iowa Hawkeyes host Penn State in a make or break game for the Nittany Lions. Make sure you catch their reports and all the weekend's college grid action Monday morning in the **Daily Collegian Sports.**

Tom Gibb's cartoon appeared in the Sept. 27, 1974 edition of *The Daily Collegian.*

Although he only managed to gain 65 yards in the 1974 31-10 loss to Penn State, Tony Dorsett assured himself of another 1,000-yard season.

The trip, in spite of a severe scolding by the paper's editor who choked on the expense vouchers, was a success. Although Dorsett managed just 59 yards in 15 rushing attempts during a 16-7 loss to Southern Cal, the *Collegian's* scouting report was favorable. The idea here was to build up the anticipated showdown between Penn State's defense and Pitt's All-American halfback exactly two months to the day after the USC game (Nov. 28).

The Pitt-Penn State game was played at night in Three Rivers Stadium for the benefit of a national television audience. But the buildup on Dorsett was a bust as Tony struggled for 65 yards and one touchdown. At least Dorsett had assured himself of another 1,000-yard season. Pitt lost, 31-10, before 45,895 as Penn State scored 25 second-half points and Chris Bahr kicked a school-record four field goals.

A good deal of the drama unfolded inside the Lion locker room prior to the game. Fullback Tom Donchez, in an effort to inspire the squad, heaved his helmet into the unsuspecting face of future All-American linebacker Greg Buttle. Buttle was knocked unconscious by the blow. Standing over Buttle's prostrate body, Coach Joe Paterno inquired aloud whether it would be possible in the future to get through the team prayer without injury.

At least Penn State got through the game without injury. Bahr booted his first field goal from 50 yards—a yard shy of Pete Mauthe's 1912 series record. Then he hit from 21 yards as Pitt held a 7-6 halftime lead on Dorsett's two-yard run plus Carson Long's PAT.

A 31-yard Bahr field goal combined with a 23-yard touchdown pass from Tom Shuman to Jim Eaise pulled Penn State in front, 16-10, in the third quarter. Eaise's score, his first of two that night, came after four successive completions that climaxed with his fly pattern past two Panther defenders.

A 38-yard Bahr field goal in the fourth quarter plus Tom Williams' end zone recovery of a fumble gave Penn State a 25-10 lead. Eaise got his second touchdown a little later, this one on a 35-yard pass from Shuman that added up to 31-10.

Eaise displayed mixed emotions after fumbling two first-half punts, the second of which resulted in a 30-yard drive and Dorsett's touchdown, Pitt's only legitimate score of the night. (Long booted a 40-yard field goal.)

"Yeah, I was feeling bad about that," Eaise said of his sudden attack of fumblitis. "The only score they got I gave 'em. Our defense had contained them both times and then they had to go right back out on the field. It (two touchdowns) was sort of atoning for myself."

Chris Bahr, two-sport letterman (soccer and football) at Penn State.

Paterno was ecstatic with Bahr's kicking. Earlier that season, Bahr lost his starting role to John Reihner when the former muffed four field goals against Navy.

"Ever have a day shooting pool," Paterno asked the media, "when bang, bang, everything goes in, then you can't make anything? Well, kicking is like that too."

Bahr, who won the James Coogan Award in this game, said he never lost sight of his ability because he knew things would work themselves out.

"That first one (50 yards) did feel good," Bahr admitted. "I never lost my confidence . . . The weather was bad, I was bad, a lot was bad back then."

Penn State humbled Baylor in the Cotton Bowl to finish 10-2 and seventh in both wire polls. Pitt continued to show signs of improvement under Majors, although Johnny wasn't satisfied with a 7-4 record.

"We got some growing pains out there tonight," Majors groaned.

And some growing pains with TV revenue, as well. Penn State took home a hefty chunk of change for its Friday night TV appearance — $243,000.

1975

Game 75

Long Night for Carson

Carson Long's wife had given birth to a baby girl only hours before her husband was to undergo the most agonizing game of his career. It was a game in which the usually trustworthy kicker missed a crucial extra point, then completely lost his poise in front of 47,000 fans at Three Rivers Stadium and millions more on TV by blowing three field goals as Pitt lost 7-6 to Penn State.

Long was absolutely devastated afterward. Two of those missed field goals in the fourth quarter came in the last minute of play. One was a 30-yarder. The other, with only three seconds on the clock, was 40. Like the one before, it was wide. Way wide.

"Did you ever need to make a three-foot putt on the 16th for a $10 Nassau?" asked Pitt Coach Johnny Majors. "Well, multiply that pressure a thousand times and you know what our guy felt. Listen, Carson Long is my friend. I respect him. All I said to him was keep your head up. I'll bet you he'd borrow whatever it took, if he had to pay back a thousand dollars a year the rest of his life, to have made any one of those kicks."

Penn State won the game because as *Philadelphia Inquirer* columnist Bill Lyon wrote, The Lions had "a second-year assistant coach who is a film freak and a defensive halfback who might make the All-World Leapfrog team." Lyon's column dealt entirely with one aspect — the key aspect — of the game: how Penn State prepared to block one of Long's PATs.

Carson Long, Pitt place-kicker.

Elliott Walker had given the Panthers a 6-0 lead in the second quarter on a bold 37-yard running play. When Pitt lined up for the extra-point attempt, Penn State's Tom Odell hurdled center and caught Long's boot smack in his chest. Imagine the surprise on Long's face. It was his first miss after 60 consecutive conversions.

Assistant coach Greg Ducatte, a former Nittany Lion, spent bleary-eyed nights watching how Pitt lined up for extra points. He concluded two things: 1) that the center kept his head very low and didn't get up right away, 2) and, that Long's kicks go a full two yards before rising. Ducatte told head coach Joe Paterno that someone who could jump high would stand a good chance of leap-frogging the center and blocking the kick. That someone was Tom Odell.

"You gotta figure all those little things," Ducatte told Lyon.

Sure enough, that's what Odell did. Long immediately knew the Lions had detected a weakness in placements and spent the remainder of the game worried it might happen again.

Ducatte figured "Odio" was the right man because the senior had high-jumped 27 inches from a stand-still position. Odio confirmed reporters' suspicions that he was part lizard by admitting he had long-jumped 24 feet in high school.

"The center pulled his elbows up and that meant it was legal for me to go," Odell explained. "At first, I thought I'd gone in too fast and too deep. I'm in the air and I'm thinking ,'Oh, no, he's gonna kick it right under me.' "

But Long's kick sliced Odio in the chest. Later, a 23-yard field attempt by Long was partially blocked by Odell. "I felt it rush by me, felt maybe I brushed it," Odell said. "Just ticked it with my little finger."

That block really jolted Long's confidence. After all, the guy was one of the best kickers in college football and here he was shanking chip shots from 23 yards away.

Penn State got its only touchdown in the fourth quarter as freshman quarterback Chuck Fusina directed a 69-yard scoring drive that ended with tailback Steve Geise's 29-yard run. Geise, too, was a frosh. His TD run, designed to pick up only a fraction of what he gained, was a slant through the line.

The role of freshman football players was well-documented by Paterno. Joe had been saying for years to anyone who would listen that freshmen belonged on the bench, not on the playing field. Perhaps Majors' use of Tony Dorsett began turning the wheels in his mind, even though Paterno would have been the last to admit it.

"Thank God, I'm stupid," Paterno said. "I don't mind eating crow about freshmen."

Speaking of Dorsett, who was a junior by now, he picked up 125 yards in 28 rushing attempts but was held scoreless.

"This is the first time since I've been here that I thought we had the confidence to beat them," Majors lamented.

"Pitt played inspired," answered Paterno. "This year, they felt they were going to beat us. I could sense that. I thought we were good enough to beat them but every time it looked like we were going to take control of the game, we'd give the ball away."

Penn State fumbled five times, losing three and Fusina threw one interception in relief of junior John Andress.

"We put Fusina in because we needed some quickness to the outside," Paterno noted. "Every time I looked up we had 80 yards to go, and we weren't moving inside."

The Lions (9-3) went on to the Sugar Bowl where they lost 13-6 to Alabama, their second bowl appearance in 1975, if you count the previous January's 41-20 win over Baylor at the Cotton Bowl which capped off the '74 season.

Majors' drive toward excellence at Pitt continued as the Panthers finished 8-4 and ripped apart Kansas, 33-19, in the Sun Bowl.

Pitt fans eagerly awaited 1976 when Dorsett would be a senior. Another guy anxious to get one last bite at the Lions was Carson Long.

1976

Game 76

Dorsett's Night

When Johnny Majors arrived at Pitt in December of 1972, he vowed to university officials that he would "do anything" to assure Pitt of a respectable football program, to bring Pitt football back into the prominence it enjoyed from 1916 through the '20s.

First order of business was recruiting. Majors had been told of a sensational kid in Aliquippa, Pa. who attended Hopewell High School. His name was Tony Dorsett. The two met, although Majors felt certain Dorsett was headed for Penn State.

"If Penn State had recruited me like I wanted to be recruited," Dorsett recalled, "I probably would have gone there. Pittsburgh, you know, they made me feel like I was very important to them."

Dorsett was not the first great player to come from that area of Western Pennsylvania. Beaver County had produced many over the years, the first being Joe Namath under the guidance of Larry Bruno in Beaver Falls. In fact, the *Geographical Review* of October 1969 cites a fascinating statistic involving counties that rank highest in the United States in output of college football players. Beaver County was second in the nation with a 3.99 per capita rate. Only Steubenville, Oh., placed more (4.66).

If you think Joe Paterno felt bad about losing Dorsett to Pitt, imagine how Don Yannessa, coach at Aliquippa, felt when he heard Tony, who lived in the town, was going to play for Yannessa's chief adversary—Butch Ross at Hopewell.

Tony Dorsett, Pitt's greatest running back.

Dorsett Proves Who's No. 1

The Philadelphia Inquirer

sports

section

C

♦♦ Saturday, Nov. 27, 1976

Pitt crushes Penn State, 24-7

Tony Dorsett scores Pitt's first touchdown in the second quarter and the Panthers went on to complete an undefeated season

Associated Press

Dorsett gains 224 scores 2

By Chuck Newman
Inquirer Staff Writer

PITTSBURGH — Penn State did not have a key linebacker, Ron Hostetler, available for last night' game against Pitt, the nation's No. 1 ranked football team. For one half, they tried to disguise the use of a freshman substitute, showing a number of defenses in an effort to deter Tony Dorsett from exploiting the weakness.

For 30 minutes it worked. Dorsett got only 58 first half yards in 16 carries. But by the end of a 24-7 Pitt victory and a perfect season (11-0), there was nothing to hide.

Dorsett became the first runner to rush 6,000 yards in a college career. He picked up 224 yards, scored two touchdowns, tied two NCAA records and set another.

The man they call "T.D." broke a 7-7 tie with a 40-yard burst up the middle at 1 minute 17 seconds of the third period and started Pitt to its first undefeated season since 1918 when it went 4-0 defeating Penn State, 28-16). The win also snapped Pitt's 10-game winless streak against the Nittany Lions.

Dorsett, leading candidate for the Heisman Trophy, recorded his 11th 100-yard game of the season, tied Archie Griffin's record of 33 100-yard

(See PITT on 2-C)

By 1976, Pitt and Dorsett had geared themselves for a run at greatness. The National Championship they craved so badly was within their grasp. The man who held fate in his palms was Tony Dorsett, who was systematically obliterating every NCAA football record in his path.

"I'll tell you what, he's the greatest," Al Romano, Pitt's middle guard, told the *Philadelphia Bulletin's* Frank Bilovsky. "It wouldn't be too far-fetched to say there'll never be another running back in college like him. He amazes us every week. I hate to practice against him. It's like trying to catch a fly."

Joe Paterno had a simpler explanation of Dorsett. "How many ways can you say great?" Paterno inquired.

And great Dorsett was on the night of Nov. 26, 1976, when he trampled all over Penn State's defense, rambling for 224 yards and two touchdowns as Pitt coasted to a 24-7 victory at Three Rivers Stadium. Even better, an entire nation had witnessed the carnage.

"I didn't think they could run up the gut like that on us," Paterno confessed. "I didn't think I'd see Dorsett at fullback. We just weren't ready for the unbalanced stuff.

"They made us look bad. They showed their class when things weren't going well for them at the beginning. We got an easy score on them but they never lost their poise.

"It's been 10 years since they beat us. I don't begrudge them a single point. If they wanted to make it 31-7, that's okay with me. It's been a long time coming and they earned it."

Majors' coaching job in this game was one of the best in series history. A Chuck Fusina-to-Bob Torrey 21-yard pass in the first quarter gave Penn State a 7-0 lead. Dorsett's six-yard run in the second quarter plus Carson Long's PAT tied it up. By the way, Long avenged his dismal 1975 performance with three extra points and a booming 47-yard field goal that clinched the win.

At the half, Majors decided to switch his fleet tailback to the fullback spot. Dorsett, playing in a new position, rushed for 173 yards in 22 carries and scored his other touchdown. Good backs don't make the transition from tailback to fullback in 12 minutes between halves. Great backs do.

"Penn State did a great job of keeping us off-balance," Majors explained. "We had three or four big plays off that I formation and I think that was the difference in the ballgame."

Dorsett's second TD heaved him over the 100-yard mark in the game, tying Archie Griffin's NCAA record for century games in a season (11) and career (33). Eliott Walker's fourth-quarter score gave Pitt its last touchdown.

When it was all over, Dorsett was the proud owner of 14 NCAA records. Among them:

–Career rushing yardage, 6,082
–Season rushing yardage, 1,948
–Career points, 356
–Most seasons gaining 1,000 yards or more, 4
–Most seasons gaining 1,500 yards or more, 3
–Career rushes, 1,074
–Career all-purpose yardage (rush, receive, runback), 6,611

Dorsett's career rushing total was the one record he was most proud of.

"There's a great possibility I put that record out of sight," said Dorsett, who according to *Philadelphia Daily News* writer Bill Conlin, looked like "the wreck of the Edmund Fitzgerald" afterward. "For a while, I didn't think I'd get untracked. That field was like ice. I couldn't make any cuts at all. Their defense the first half confused us. And they were hitting like crazy."

Paterno informed Dorsett that the Nittany Lion coach would be the main speaker at the Heisman dinner which would honor him as that year's award winner.

"I told Tony, 'I'll give you a call to see what you want me to say about you,' " Paterno told everyone.

"I'm not sure I like him gaining all those yards against Penn State," Joe continued, "but I hope he gets 400 against Georgia."

Georgia. The Sugar Bowl. New Orleans. National Championship on the line.

Pitt had not won a national title since 1937 when Jock Sutherland staked his claim with a 9-0-1 Panther squad. In fact, the last national champ from the East was Ben Schwartzwalder's 1959 Syracuse team.

Pitt went to New Orleans and humbled Georgia, 27-3, as Dorsett rushed for 202 yards, breaking Eddie Prokop's (Georgia Tech) record of 199 set in 1944 against Tulsa. Because the MVP voting was collected at the half with Pitt leading 21-0, quarterback Matt Cavanaugh got the award.

The Eastern football establishment hailed Pitt as No. 1 even though Ricky Bell and Southern Cal were demanding they were better. Pitt, however, with its sterling 12-0 record was the unanimous choice in the final wire polls.

Did Majors ever think he'd be No. 1?

"In my wildest dreams, yes," Majors replied. "Because sometimes I think you do have wild dreams. I think that keeps you going."

Matt Cavanaugh, Pitt quarterback.

After the game, Majors held a quiet team meeting, told his players how proud he was to have coached a Number One team, and that he had decided to leave Pitt for Tennessee. In time, Jackie Sherrill would be named his successor.

Dorsett confessed that he was never so primed for a football game as his very last in college.

"A lot of Bulldawg fans were staying where we were," Dorsett said. "One of the things that helped psyche us up—I really don't think their fans realized what they were doing—they were sort of agitating us . . . We didn't like it and the Dawgs. We wanted to get ahead and show the Georgia Bulldawgs who was the dog food."

Just like Pitt had done to Penn State.

1977

Game 77

A Matter of Inches

Elliott Walker was virtually in a trance. His frozen breath repeatedly spewed out the same words in the Pitt dressing room. "I got over, I got over . . ."

The successor to Tony Dorsett had failed by 10 inches to clear the goal line on a two-point conversion with Pitt trailing 15-13 at Pittsburgh. As the last 12 seconds ticked away, all Walker could hear was the referee's whistle.

"I felt one guy hit me and I stretched 'out," Walker said. "The officials blew the whistle real fast."

It was an exciting game from start to finish played in subzero temperatures, gale force winds and icy conditions at Pitt Stadium. Players said the field was more like a skating pond than turf. The kind of playing conditions that would have normally been an ally to Pitt as the Panthers had grown accustomed to the icy frost of November in the Steel City.

For Walker, the game held a special kind of disappointment. He needed just 94 yards to become the second Panther in history to climax 1,000 yards on the season. Dorsett, naturally, had done it some years earlier, then repeated the task for the remainder of his four-year stay at Pitt.

Walker was not alone in his frustration. Panther quarterback Matt Cavanaugh took the loss personally, blaming himself for failing to provide victory. Cavanaugh refused to accept the premise that the weather was a contributing factor.

Mike Guman, shown in action in a game played earlier in the season, returned a punt 52 yards for a score—a play that in the words of Pitt Coach Jackie Sherrill "decided the game".

Jackie Sherrill, Pitt Head Coach, 1977-1981.

"I'm upset with the way I played," he said. "I don't think I threw a good pass all day. And don't blame the weather. (Chuck) Fusina had a good day, didn't he?"

Yes, he did. The Nittany Lion signal caller completed 13 of 27 passes for 146 yards and two interceptions. Cavanaugh was 14 of 19 for 204 yards, but two of his three interceptions came at the most inopportune moments. One theft occurred with Pitt at the Lion 9-yard line in the first half. His second was far more costly. With less than four minutes in the game, Lion linebacker Ron Hostetler intercepted Cavanaugh in the end zone.

"I didn't think I'd get another chance," Cavanaugh said of that mistake. But Pitt's defense gave him one final try in the closing minutes.

He took the Gator Bowl-bound Panthers 53 yards on three passes in 22 seconds to come within a two-point conversion of tying the game. Pitt had trailed 15-7 until split end Gordon Jones caught a 17-yard strike cutting it to 15-13.

Penn State placed the first points on the board on Matt Bahr's 34-yard field goal. Matt, in case you haven't guessed, is Chris' younger brother. Cavanaugh's one-yard plunge forged Pitt into the lead, 7-3, following Mark Schubert's kick. Late in the second quarter, Bahr hit from 31 yards and Mike Guman returned a punt 52 yards for another score which gave Penn State a 12-7 lead.

Although Guman's punt return TD was not a series record, it may have been the cutest. Guman took it off a reverse with flanker Jimmy Cefalo.

"It was that play which decided the game," insisted Pitt's rookie coach, Jackie Sherrill. "That double reverse (sic) punt return. But we missed some tackles that made it work."

Cefalo claimed Penn State had actually worked on the play during the week of practice prior to the game. "We kept saying if we got a chance we were going to use it," Cefalo said.

Bahr's 20-yard field goal with 3:32 remaining accounted for Penn State's last points and it appeared that was all the Lions would need. As things turned out, they needed another typical Penn State goal line stand.

Fusina played with cool aplomb which, under normal circumstances, wouldn't be saying much. Except he had received three telephone calls threatening his life—and his mother's—that week. Fusina's mother told her son to ignore the crank calls, go to Pittsburgh and win.

Which is just what he had done.

Penn State Coach Joe Paterno said he had goose bumps after

the game and not because of the weather. The final seconds had been a déjà vu for Paterno. There was Pitt driving down the field behind the brilliant passing of Cavanaugh. There was Jones clutching the pass that brought Pitt to within two points of a tie. And there was the final goal line stand as Pitt tried to tie it on the conversion, while the clock expired.

"This game was as exciting as the Orange Bowl game we played against Kansas," Paterno said of that 1969 thriller when the Lions pulled off a 15-14 victory on a two-pointer with no time on the clock.

"I've been coming to Pitt Stadium for 28 years and this win could be the sweetest."

This was the first of five interesting encounters between Paterno and Sherrill, who is the only coach in Eastern football to inherit a National Champion. Sherrill had been a major force behind Pitt's recruiting from the time he joined Majors' staff as an assistant in 1973. He left following the '75 season to coach Washington State (3-8) but gladly accepted a return invitation as Pitt's head man when Majors went to Tennessee.

This game had been a battle for Eastern supremacy. Penn State (11-1) went on to rout Arizona State, 42-30, in the Fiesta Bowl, and finished fifth in the polls. Pitt (9-2-1) embarrassed Clemson, 34-3, at the Gator and was ranked eighth.

Strange, but true, Pitt placed four men on the All-America team — Cavanaugh, Randy Holloway (T), Bob Jury (S) and Tom Brzoza (C). What is odd is that Pitt placed only two men on that same squad a year earlier when it won the National Championship.

Penn State's Keith Dorney (DT) and Randy Sidler (MG) both made All-American in 1977.

1978

Game 78

Fusina Fibbed

Joe Paterno was getting all sorts of information, none of which made sense. Four yards, no three, wait a minute, maybe it's two. Oh, why not go look for yourself. He couldn't, of course, and sent Chuck Fusina in his place.

Fusina went onto the dark Beaver Stadium field Nov. 24, 1978 and saw that Penn State needed some yardage on its fourth down play, trailing Pitt, 10-7. Joe would have preferred to kick, get the tie, but his Lions were ranked No.1 in the land and as such, had to do something better than settle for a tie with only five minutes left in the game.

Fusina reported back to his coach that the distance wasn't insurmountable. The Nittany Lion quarterback held his hands two feet apart. Paterno had already sent Matt Bahr out for what would have amounted to a chip shot field goal try (21 yards). Joe called him back.

"I wanted to go for it," Paterno would later say. "You can't say you're No. 1 if you're willing to settle for a tie."

Of course, Paterno didn't know that Penn State needed more than two feet, more like two yards, for that first down.

"I lied a little," Fusina smirked.

"I just wanted us to score. A touchdown, I mean. Run or pass, I didn't care. Just so it was a touchdown. You can't be No. 1 by playing for a tie."

Chuck Fusina, Penn State quarterback.

So, the Lions went for it. The play was a pitchback to Mike Guman, who knifed through a hole neatly carved out by tackle Keith Dorney and tight end Ive Pankey, then slanted to the outside. Eric Cunningham, who was pulling on the play from his guard spot, mowed down a linebacker and Guman scissored inside for the touchdown that gave Penn State a 14-10 lead. And the game, too, though the final was 17-10.

"It's the kind of play where you just look for a crack," Guman said. "Which way you cut is determined by how the block is made."

The key men involved, Cunningham and Dorney, seemed confused with the play but somehow managed to pull it off.

"I don't really know what happened," Dorney said. "Eric pulled on that play? Oh, yeah, that's right. Well, what the heck, it worked."

"I don't know who I blocked," said Cunningham. "I chopped a guy down and we were lying there on the ground and then I heard the crowd roar."

It was a bold move, but it worked. Besides, like Fusina said, you don't play for a tie when No. 1 is on the line.

The victory preserved the Lions' 19-game winning streak and sent them to the Sugar Bowl to battle Alabama for the National Championship. But let's retrace the steps of how they got there, ending with the Pitt game.

Penn State came into the game averaging nearly 400 yards of offense, but could garner only 230 against Jackie Sherrill's Panthers. The Lion defense was tops in the nation against the run. Only Syracuse had stomped for 100 yards against Penn State. Pitt mustered 87. In other words, this game was a defensive struggle of classic proportions.

The Panthers had only themselves to blame for failing to spoil Penn State's 11-0 season. Pitt turned the ball over six times, four through interceptions, while Penn State converted those miscues into 10 points.

When sophomore quarterback Rick Trocano took to the air after Guman's TD, Penn State was ready for him. Rich Milot picked off his pass, intended for Gordon Jones, then returned it 17 yards to the Pitt 26. Bahr kicked his record 22nd field goal of the season for a 17-10 lead.

Linebacker Lance Mehl staved off Pitt's final drive with an interception, then Penn State ran the clock down to preserve the victory.

A Trocano fumble at his 15-yard line in the first quarter was directly responsible for Guman's early touchdown of three yards. Battling whirlpool-type winds, Trocano fired four consecutive completions the following series which culminated with Steve Gaustad's 16-yard end zone reception that tied the game at 7-7.

Mark Schubert banged home a 17-yard field goal midway into the third quarter as Pitt took a 10-7 lead. With the darkness overhead and chilly winds confronting the players, Pitt seemed to be in good shape provided it kept Bahr out of range.

But Fusina's fib and Paterno's reluctance to settle for a tie changed all that. It reminded you again of the 1969 Orange Bowl game when Penn state elected to run a two-point conversion against Kansas rather than settle for a tie. But those who know Paterno will also tell you that's a long wait in-between gambles.

Several records fell that season. Bahr set four kicking records while Fusina notched a career and school-high passing percentage mark of .558.

Penn State went to the Sugar Bowl where the entire stage had been set for the school's first national title. Pennsylvanians had waited so long for this opportunity, suffered through the agony of watching Penn State go 11-0 in 1968, 11-0 in 1969 and 12-0 in 1973, each time failing to capture college football's Holy Grail. Although it's difficult to justify picking Penn State No. 1 on all three occasions, Eastern writers felt they were deserving of it in 1968 or 1969.

That, however, was past history. Their moment of intended glory was now, Jan. 1, 1979 in New Orleans. With seven minutes to play, trailing 14-7, Penn State drove to the Crimson Tide's 1-yard line. What happened thereafter has been duly recorded in Lion history as The Longest Yard.

'Bama linebacker Barry Krauss and tackle Marty Lyons held their own against Matt Suhey and Guman thereby assuring the distinction between National Champions and also-rans.

The game was one of Paterno's worst in terms of playcalling; the daring, liberal attack that had carried Penn State so far that season was absent in this one. Some say, with justification, that Bear Bryant simply outcoached Paterno.

1979
Game 79

Scales Tip in Pitt's Favor

As the '70s drew to a close, the series seemed to tie in favor of Pitt, even though Penn State held a 39-36-3 edge on the Panthers. Indications that the Panthers were gaining a stronger foothold in Pennsylvania had begun with Johnny Majors, then continued with the arrival of Jackie Sherrill, easily the best recruiter the school ever had.

Recruiting says a lot about the club and where it's headed. Pitt drew the cream of the crop in the late '70s with players such as Gordon Jones, Randy McMillan, Randy Holloway, Hugh Green and Dan Marino. That's not to imply Penn State didn't with its All-America Monster Mash tackles, Bruce Clark and Matt Millen.

Folklore says the winner of the Pitt-Penn State game can usually count on signing the best athletes from Western Pennsylvania. There is no scientific evidence to back that claim up, but it is true that some kids who are wavering will make their decision based on that game.

One thing was certain as the series headed into the '80s. Penn State held a 67-7 padlock against Eastern independents and lost only four games to those respective schools. Lost twice to Pitt and once to Navy and Syracuse.

Dan Marino, Pitt quarterback, as a freshman was one of the nation's passing leaders with 1,500 yards, 1979.

Pitt football was on the rise, however, as the Panthers won more games than Penn State over the last four years of the decade (40-37), although if you compare both logs from the time Majors came on board to the close of the '70s, Penn State held the upper hand, 68-61.

Philadelphia Inquirer columnist Bill Lyon wrote of the gradual shift in power from the central part of the state to the west by comparing Joe Paterno's domain to a castle that had fallen. "The kingdom that Penn State ruled so effortlessly has shrunk considerably," Lyon wrote. "The Nittany Lion empire is being overrun by those Pitt hordes from the west."

As Pitt invaded what Penn State students lightly refer to as "Happy Valley" on Dec. 1, 1979, it brought with it a Top 10 ranking and 10-1 record.

Lyon captured the gut feeling of many who followed Pitt's program during the mediocre '60s, to the struggling-for-recognition '70s:

> At every turn, it seemed, Pitt faced the same barrier in its quest to be No.1 in the East.
>
> Always, there was Penn State. Rich, established, powerful Penn State.
>
> Yesterday, in brilliant cold, Pitt completed its insurrection. The Establishment was toppled.
>
> Pitt plundered Penn State, 29-14, and even those figures do not reveal the total dominance of the Panthers.

There had been bigger romps in the series, but few were executed with the Samurai precision displayed by Pitt in this game. Pitt savagely attacked Penn State's once-vaunted defense, then raped it for 464 yards. The Panthers' phenomenal freshman quarterback, Dan Marino, the pride of Central Catholic High, ravaged the Lion secondary for 279 yards on 17 of 31 passing efficiency. Marino's total was the most passing yards by a Panther quarterback in the series since Dave Havern polluted the air with an all-time 314 in 1968.

Marino finished the season with over 1,500 aerial yards, putting him among the nation's passing leaders. Paterno later admitted that losing Marino to Pitt had been a terrible recruiting blow.

Pitt's defense, which was ranked fourth in the country, limited Penn State to 237 yards, 30 more than the Panthers would normally yield. Hugh Green, who was the single-most dominant Pitt lineman between 1978-80, recorded three sacks. His mates had a collective three themselves.

"They owned the line of scrimmage," Paterno said. "That was the deciding factor. They knocked us off the ball."

Matt Suhey gave Penn State a brief 7-0 lead in the first quarter on

The strain of Pitt's 29-14 victory can be seen on the Penn State sideline.

Even the hard running of Booker Moore, the 7th all-time rushing leader for Penn State, was not sufficient to deny Pitt in the 1979 game.

his 65-yard touchdown run. Pitt's Mark Schubert kicked a 26-yard field goal later and that's where it stood heading into the decisive second period, a period where Pitt would score 20 points to take control of the game.

Sandwiched between two short-yardage TD runs by Randy Mc-Millan (114 yards overall, three TDs) was Curt Warner's 95-yard kickoff return, the longest Lion TD off a placement in the series since Larry Joe's 90-yarder in 1942. Two more Schubert field goals from 33 and 41 yards gave Pitt its 23-14 halftime lead.

Neither team scored in the third quarter, but a nifty 50-yard strike from Marino to McMillan in the final period provided Pitt's final six points.

If, in Lyon's estimation, the castle had finally been toppled, then it comes as no surprise that Pitt ended yet another Penn State streak. Ricky Jackson's block of Ralph Giacomarro's punt was the first since Penn State's 1969 opener. Up till then, the Lions had routinely executed 629 consecutive punts.

"This," Jackie Sherrill promised, "is the biggest win for us since the 1976 National Championship."

Pitt, unfortunately, couldn't take its glorious record and prized victory very far. Although it edged Arizona 16-10 in the Fiesta Bowl, that bowl simply didn't command the respect of the biggies (although it now commands more). Pitt finished 11-1 ranked fourth in both wire polls.

Penn State limped to Memphis, Tenn., where it struggled past Tulane, 9-7, to capture the Liberty Bowl. Penn State's 8-4 record was the "poorest" since 1976 when it went 7-5.

1980

Game 80

Good Defense,
Bad Calls

Hugh Green, Pitt's three-time All-American defensive end, called it "a double Excedrin game." "Lot of pounding, lots of limping and headaches afterwards," Green said.

Joe Paterno probably had the worst headache as the Lions' coach blew two calls in the 80th meeting between these two clubs which ultimately cost Penn State the game. On an afternoon so cold, tears fell as icicles, Pitt claimed a 14-9 victory before 82,459 at Beaver Stadium.

The media seemed split on how to judge this one. One faction felt it had been a great defensive game with the better defensive club winning. The other agreed with the first part of that assessment but arrived at a different conclusion. Pitt had won because Paterno tried two fancy fourth down plays instead of sticking to basic football, they argued.

Judge for yourself: Penn State was trailing, 14-9, in the middle of the fourth quarter with the ball at the Panther 15-yard line. Fourth-and-one. Tailback Joel Coles, who had thrown only two option passes for touchdowns that season, swept right. It was his choice either to run or throw, depending upon the "read" he got from Pitt's defense. Coles elected to run . . . right into the waiting bearhug of Green. No gain.

Hugh Green, Pitt All-American, won the Maxwell Award and Lombardi Trophy, 1980.

Jackie Sherrill and his quarterback, Dan Marino.

With four minutes left, Penn State faced a similar fourth down situation at the Pitt 36. Another sweep play. Quarterback Todd Blackledge is hurried by Pitt's onrushing lineman and pitches too soon to Curt Warner. Warner is nailed by Ricky Jackson and Carlton Williamson for a two-yard loss.

Why Paterno ignored the simple, obvious solution of using full-back Booker Moore up the middle was the bone of contention here.

"Pitt made up their mind that they wouldn't let us run," Paterno said. "They are some of the best people we have played against. They are so experienced that it's tough to get them out of certain patterns or situations.

"They made the big plays when they had to . . . It's awfully tough to make a long drive on them."

Pitt came up with one more big play when Williamson intercepted a Blackledge pass in the final minute to smother the Lions' last gasp for victory. What hurt even more is all Blackledge was trying to do was stop the clock. Williamson stopped everything.

"You saw something today," said Lion linebacker Chet Parlavecchio. "You saw the two best defensive teams in the country."

Pitt, ranked fourth in the wire polls, threw for 143 yards, well-below Rick Trocano's usual big-game stats. The week before, junior Dan Marino came off the injury list to throw for a personal high 292 yards against Army. Pitt's greatest offensive weapon—its quarter-backs' arms—hung limp against Penn State.

The fifth-ranked Lions had averaged over 200 yards in nine of their 10 games, the notable exception coming against Nebraska which mocked those fancy stats by holding Penn State to 33 yards on 40 attempts. Against Pitt, Penn State squirmed its way to 105 yards. Some say, that's why Paterno deviated from the norm on fourth down and tried something unexpected.

Pitt held a 7-3 lead at the half on Trocano's 16-yard scoring pass to Benjie Pryor, the Panthers' excellent tight end from Valley High. Herb Menhardt's 27-yard field goal in the first quarter gave Penn State its only lead in the game.

Trocano's nine-yard run in the third period made it 14-3, then Blackledge hit flanker Kenny Jackson with a 13-yard scoring pass to bring Penn State to within 14-9. Thinking field goal as a possible tie at the end, Penn State attempted a two-point conversion, but Black-ledge's pass failed.

Everyone lauded Pitt's defense. Middle guard Jerry Boyarsky was virtually impregnable. The pitches and sweeps Penn State attempted on the flanks met a similar fate at the hands of Green and Ricky Jackson. Green later said he had played the game with a badly sprained ankle.

"The difference," Jackson offered, "was we controlled the line of

Joe Paterno

scrimmage. We want the middle blocked up, and Hugh and I have enough speed to run down any of the backs."

Nothing like playing with an abundance of confidence, eh?

"We tell the big guys inside to block it up and me and Ricky will take anything that bounces outside," Green added. "Games are won on defense. But I'll tell you, Penn State has a good offensive line."

Not good enough, in Paterno's estimation, however, to risk a fourth down gut rush, the difference between winning and losing in this one.

"I thought it was a great football game; Pitt deserves an awful lot of credit," Paterno said.

Of particular note that season was Lion punter Ralph Giacomarro's new record of 43.3 yards per kick for a season average. The old record (41.4) was set by Chuck Raisig in 1962.

Penn State went on to crush Ohio State, 31-9, at the Fiesta Bowl. The Lions (10-2) finished eight in the polls. Pitt rolled over South Carolina, 37-9, at the Gator Bowl. The Panthers's 11-1 record was good enough for second place in the wire polls. Had Pitt not lost 36-22 to Florida State earlier in the season, it would have undoubtedly won the National Championship.

1981

Game 81

No. 1 Dream Shattered

His eyes were red. The tears had evaporated by now, but not the hurt Sal Sunseri was feeling inside. The awful pain which accompanies an embarrassing day on a football field. The agony of losing badly to Penn State.

"It gets to a point," said the Pitt linebacker, "that you don't know what to do to stop it."

Stop the 31-14 rout from getting larger. Pitt couldn't. Penn State, the team that choked when the big ones were on the line, pulverized No. 1 Pitt, 48-14, on Nov. 28, 1981 at Pitt Stadium.

Earlier in the season, Penn State, ranked No. 1 for ever so brief a moment, was upset at Miami. The ranking was gone and wouldn't return. Oh, sure, Joe Paterno's boys got a chance to reclaim it. But a 31-16 loss to Alabama—Bear Bryant's 314th victory, tying him with Amos Alonzo Stagg—permanently sealed the magic portal to the top.

As Penn State fell, Pitt rose. All the way to Number One with a 10-0 record as it hosted 8-2 Penn State on an otherwise perfect afternoon of football in Western Pennsylvania.

No one imagined that Penn State would upset Pitt. The Panthers finished second in the nation in 1980 and even though they lost Hugh Green—among others—Jackie Sherrill felt confident this team would be right up in the thick of it when New Year's rolled around.

Todd Blackledge, Penn State quarterback.

Sean Farrell, Penn State guard, scored a touchdown on a fumble recovery, 1981.

Pitt blistered its '81 opponents, gaining momentum every week until the fateful showdown against its dreaded arch-rival. Always, there was Penn State, remember?

Said *Philadelphia Inquirer* columnist Bill Lyon, ". . . it was sweet vindication for a coach who has been pillorized for Stone Age play calling . . ."

Sugar Bowl representative Henry Bodenheimer, who was scouting the team which would play Georgia, presumably for the National Championship, remarked, "This is unreal. I can hardly believe it."

Well, believe this. Sophomore quarterback Todd Blackledge completed 12 of 23 passes for 262 yards. Classmate Kenny Jackson caught two of those passes, both for touchdowns, equaling two school records: TD receptions one season (6); career TD receptions (11). His 158 yards (five receptions) broke Jack Curry's 1965 record of 148 against California.

Both passes, the first 42 yards, the second three yards farther, catapulted Penn State from a 14-4 third quarter deadlock to a 28-14 lead.

"Maybe we didn't pay enough attention to him," said Panther safety Tom Flynn, who called the defensive signals. "We sort of thought he was having a bad year, and he stuck it in our face."

And Curt Warner stuck it to Pitt's defensive line, rushing for 104 yards on 21 carries. Oddly enough, the junior tailback did not score in this game. But enough others did to more than make up for his missing share of the workload.

Fullback Mike Meade scored on a two-yard run in the second quarter with Penn State trailing 14-0. Blackledge's eight-yard run tied it at 14-14. Both Panther scores were the result of Dan Marino hurling touchdown passes of 28 and nine yards to flanker Dwight Collins in the first quarter.

Following Jackson's two TD receptions, a 39-yard Brian Franco field goal expanded Penn State's lead to 31-14, heading into a humiliating fourth quarter in which Paterno's boys sledgehammered 17 more points on the board.

Warner got within a yard of what would have been his only touchdown of the afternoon, then fumbled the ball. A series of "dolphin flips," according to the *Inquirer's* Bill Livingston, ensued, and offensive guard Sean Farrell recovered in the end zone for his first touchdown since high school.

"You *know* I wanted to spike the ball," Farrell giggled.

Mark Robinson concluded Pitt's worst series mugging since 1971 (55-18) by returning one of Marino's errant passes 91 yards for a touchdown. The distance covered on the theft qualified for a series

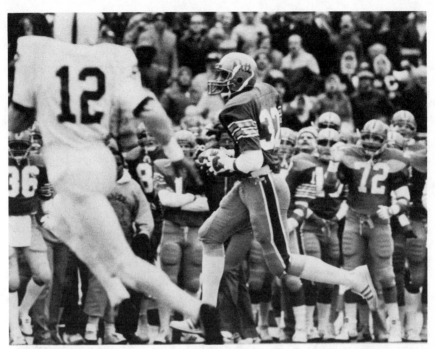

Dwight Collins, Pitt halfback, had two touchdown receptions in the 1981 game.

Kenny Jackson, Penn State end, caught two touchdown passes against Pitt, 1981.

Curt Warner, Penn State halfback, rushed for 104 yards in the 1981 game.

record.

Nittany Lion linebacker Chet Parlavecchio said the game offered a refresher course in catch-up football.

"We had practiced coming from behind," Parlavecchio said. "When you play teams that roll over every week, you're not used to coming back. You don't know how."

Flynn was asked what bothered Pitt's player most about the loss. Losing the No. 1 spot in the polls, watching a 17-game unbeaten streak end, or spoiling Jackie Sherrill's 38th birthday?

"None of those," Flynn replied bitterly. "It's losing to Penn State."

Epilogue

Penn State finished 10-2 and third in both polls after toying with Southern Cal, 26-10, at the Fiesta Bowl. Pitt was 11-1 and even though it didn't give the Sugar Bowl a fifth national championship game in six years, it supplied a gutty 24-20 come-from-behind upset over Georgia.

As of 1981, Penn State held a 40-38 lead in the series, with three ties. The Lions also owned the scoreboard, chalking up 1,246 points to Pitt's 1,055.

The biggest turnaround in the series was between 1960-80 when Penn State flip-flopped a 24-33 deficit into a 39-38 lead. Coincidentally, during the two decades in which the series took its most dramatic shift, Pitt went through five coaches. Penn State went through two, but its only changing of the guard—from Rip Engle to Joe Paterno—was accomplished via retirement, not firing.

Obviously, a glance at the series standings shows there is no clear-cut Beast of the East reigning the hills of Pennsylvania at the moment. One year it's Pitt, the next Penn State. Football fans in the Keystone State say that's what makes this collegiate series so exciting. The balance of power is equally distributed from the sleepy town of State College to the urban mass of Pittsburgh.

If the future is anything like the past, The Beast of the East will rear its head for years to come in quest of increased recognition, bowl bids and National Championships.

REFERENCES

Cromartie, Bill. *Michigan vs. Ohio State, The Big One.* West Point: Leisure Press, 1981.

Michener, James A. *Sports in America.* New York: Random House, 1976.

Riley, Ridge. *Road to Number One.* New York: Doubleday, 1977.

OTHER SOURCES

Collier's Encyclopedia. New York: 1961.

Illustrated World Encyclopedia. New York: 1977.

CBS News Almanac. New Jersey: 1978.

NEWSPAPERS

Philadelphia *Bulletin*, 1950-1982.

Philadelphia *Daily News*, 1976-1982.

Philadelphia *Inquirer*, 1920-1982.

Philadelphia *Journal*, 1980.

Pittsburgh *Post-Gazette*, 1893-1950.

Pittsburgh *Press*, 1893-1950.

Pittsburgh *Sun-Telegraph*, 1935, 1950.

STUDENT PUBLICATIONS

The Daily Collegian. Penn State University, 1973-74.

Appendix

RECORDS SECTION

COMPLETE PITT vs. PENN STATE SERIES, 1893-1981

G	YEAR-DATE		PLACE	WINNER	SCORE	SERIES STAND-INGS
1	1893	(Nov. 6)	State College	Penn State	32-0	1- 0, PSU
2	1896	(Oct. 3)	State College	Penn State	10- 4	2- 0
3	1900	(Sept. 29)	State College	Penn State	12- 0	3- 0
4	1901	(Sept. 29)	State College	Penn State	36-0	4- 0
5	1902	(Sept. 27)	State College	Penn State	27- 0	5- 0
6	1903	(Oct. 24)	Pittsburgh	Penn State	59- 0	6- 0
7	1904	(Nov. 24)	Pittsburgh	Pitt	22- 5	6- 1
8	1905	(Nov. 30)	Pittsburgh	Penn State	6- 0	7- 1
9	1906	(Nov. 29)	Pittsburgh	Penn State	6- 0	8- 1
10	1907	(Nov. 28)	Pittsburgh	Pitt	6- 0	8- 2
11	1908	(Nov. 26)	Pittsburgh	Penn State	12- 6	9- 2
12	1909	(Nov. 25)	Pittsburgh	Penn State	5- 0	10- 2
13	1910	(Nov. 24)	Pittsburgh	Pitt	11- 0	10- 3
14	1911	(Nov. 30)	Pittsburgh	Penn State	3- 0	11- 3
15	1912	(Nov. 28)	Pittsburgh	Penn State	38- 0	12- 3
16	1913	(Nov. 27)	Pittsburgh	Pitt	7- 6	12- 4
17	1914	(Nov. 26)	Pittsburgh	Pitt	13- 3	12- 5
18	1915	(Nov. 25)	Pittsburgh	Pitt	20- 0	12- 6
19	1916	(Nov. 30)	Pittsburgh	Pitt	31- 0	12- 7
20	1917	(Nov. 29)	Pittsburgh	Pitt	28- 6	12- 8
21	1918	(Nov. 28)	Pittsburgh	Pitt	28- 6	12- 9
22	1919	(Nov. 27)	Pittsburgh	Penn State	20- 0	13- 9
23	1920	(Nov. 25)	Pittsburgh	Tie	0- 0	13- 9-1
24	1921	(Nov. 24)	Pittsburgh	Tie	0- 0	13- 9-2
25	1922	(Nov. 30)	Pittsburgh	Pitt	14- 0	13-10-2
26	1923	(Nov. 29)	Pittsburgh	Pitt	20- 3	13-11-2
27	1924	(Nov. 27)	Pittsburgh	Pitt	24- 3	13-12-2
28	1925	(Nov. 26)	Pittsburgh	Pitt	23- 7	13-13-2
29	1926	(Nov. 25)	Pittsburgh	Pitt	24- 6	13-14-2
30	1927	(Nov. 24)	Pittsburgh	Pitt	30- 0	13-15-2
31	1928	(Nov. 29)	Pittsburgh	Pitt	26- 0	13-16-2
32	1929	(Nov. 28)	Pittsburgh	Pitt	20- 7	13-17-2
33	1930	(Nov. 27)	Pittsburgh	Pitt	19-12	13-18-2
34	1931	(Oct. 31)	State College	Pitt	41- 6	13-19-2
35	1935	(Oct. 26)	Pittsburgh	Pitt	9- 0	13-20-2
36	1936	(Nov. 7)	Pittsburgh	Pitt	34- 7	13-21-2
37	1937	(Nov. 20)	Pittsburgh	Pitt	28- 7	13-22-2

38	1938	(Nov. 19)	Pittsburgh	Pitt	26- 0	13-23-2
39	1939	(Nov. 25)	State College	Penn State	10- 0	14-23-2
40	1940	(Nov. 23)	Pittsburgh	Pitt	20- 7	14-24-2
41	1941	(Nov. 22)	Pittsburgh	Penn State	31- 7	15-24-2
42	1942	(Nov. 21)	State College	Penn State	14- 6	16-24-2
43	1943	(Nov. 20)	Pittsburgh	Penn State	14- 0	17-24-2
44	1944	(Nov. 25)	Pittsburgh	Pitt	14- 0	17-25-2
45	1945	(Nov. 24)	Pittsburgh	Pitt	7- 0	17-26-2
46	1946	(Nov. 23)	Pittsburgh	Pitt	14- 7	17-27-2
47	1947	(Nov. 22)	Pittsburgh	Penn State	29- 0	18-27-2
48	1948	(Nov. 20)	Pittsburgh	Pitt	7- 0	18-28-2
49	1949	(Nov. 19)	Pittsburgh	Pitt	19- 0	18-29-2
50	1950	(Dec. 2)	Pittsburgh	Penn State	21-20	19-29-2
51	1951	(Nov. 24)	Pittsburgh	Pitt	13- 7	19-30-2
52	1952	(Nov. 22)	Pittsburgh	Penn State	17- 0	20-30-2
53	1953	(Nov. 21)	Pittsburgh	Penn State	17- 0	21-30-2
54	1954	(Nov. 20)	Pittsburgh	Penn State	13- 0	22-30-2
55	1955	(Nov. 19)	State College	Pitt	20- 0	22-31-2
56	1956	(Nov. 24)	Pittsburgh	Tie	7- 7	22-31-3
57	1957	(Nov. 23)	Pittsburgh	Pitt	14-13	22-32-3
58	1958	(Nov. 27)	Pittsburgh	Penn State	25-21	23-32-3
59	1959	(Nov. 21)	Pittsburgh	Pitt	22- 7	23-33-3
60	1960	(Nov. 19)	Pittsburgh	Penn State	14- 3	24-33-3
61	1961	(Nov. 25)	Pittsburgh	Penn State	47-26	25-33-3
62	1962	(Nov. 24)	Pittsburgh	Penn State	16- 0	26-33-3
63	1963	(Dec. 7)	Pittsburgh	Pitt	22-21	26-34-3
64	1964	(Nov. 21)	State College	Penn State	28- 0	27-34-3
65	1965	(Nov. 20)	Pittsburgh	Pitt	30-27	27-35-3
66	1966	(Nov. 19)	Pittsburgh	Penn State	48-24	28-35-3
67	1967	(Nov. 25)	State College	Penn State	42- 6	29-35-3
68	1968	(Nov. 23)	Pittsburgh	Penn State	65- 9	30-35-3
69	1969	(Nov. 22)	Pittsburgh	Penn State	27- 7	31-35-3
70	1970	(Nov. 21)	State College	Penn State	35-15	32-35-3
71	1971	(Nov. 20)	Pittsburgh	Penn State	55-18	33-35-3
72	1972	(Nov. 25)	State College	Penn State	49-27	34-35-3

PENN STATE INDIVIDUAL SCORING
1893-1981

PLAYER	TD	PAT	FG	TOTAL	YEAR(S) SCORED
Abbey, Don	5	7	0	37	1967-68-69
*Abromitis, Bill	1	0	0	6	1943
Alter, Spike	1	0	0	6	1937
Anders, Paul	2	0	0	12	1950
Arnelle, Jesse	1	0	0	6	1951
Atherton, Charles	1	5	0	14	1893
Bahr, Chris	0	5	6	23	1973-74-75
Bahr, Matt	0	2	4	14	1977-78
Bailey, Don	1	0	0	6	1954

PLAYER	TD	PAT	FG	TOTAL	YEAR(S) SCORED
Bennett, Robert	1	0	0	4	1901
Berryman, Punk	1	0	0	6	1912
Blackledge, Todd	1	0	0	6	1981
Bland, Dave	1	0	0	6	1972
Botula, Pat	1	0	0	6	1958
Burkhart, Chuck	(see Series Touchdown Passes)				
Buzin, Rich	1	0	0	6	1967
Campbell, Bobby	3	1	0	20	1966
Capozzoli, Tony	0	1	0	1	1976
Cappelletti, John	1	0	0	6	1973
Caprara, Babe	0	1	0	1	1957
Caum, Don	1	0	0	6	1963
Caye, Eddie	(see Series Touchdown Passes)				
Cenci, Aldo	1	0	0	6	1942
Clark, John	1	0	0	6	1913
Coates, Ron	0	4	1	7	1962-63
Conover, Larry	1	0	0	6	1917
Cooper, Mike	(see Series Touchdown Passes)				
Cubbage, Bob	0	2	0	2	1919
Cummings, Ralph	1	0	0	4	1900
Curry, Jack	2	1	0	13	1966-67
Czekaj, Ed	0	5	1	8	1943-46-47
Debes, Gary	1	0	0	6	1971
Diedrich, Yutz	0	1	0	1	1929
Dunsmore, J. A.	2	0	0	8	1896
Dunsmore, William	1	0	0	4	1893
Eaise, Jim	2	0	0	12	1974
Edwards, Earle	1	0	0	6	1930
Ensminger,	0	1	0	2	1896
Farrell, Sean	1	0	0	6	1981
Forkum, Carl	6	9	0	43	1902-03
Franco, Brian	0	6	2	12	1981
Fusina, Chuck	(see Series Touchdown Passes)				
Ganter, Fran	2	0	0	12	1968-70
Garrity, Jim	0	3	1	6	1953-54
Garthwaite, Bob	0	7	1	10	1968
Geise, Steve	1	0	0	6	1975
Gingrich, Dick	0	2	0	2	1964
Guman, Mike	3	0	0	18	1977-78
Gursky, Al	3	0	0	18	1961-62
Haley, Ed	2	0	0	8	1893
Hall, Butch	2	0	0	12	1961
Harris, Franco	5	0	0	30	1969-70-71
Harrison, Harry	1	0	0	6	1936
Hayes, Dave	0	1	0	2	1960
Hayman, Gary	2	1	0	14	1972-73

INDIVIDUAL SCORING (Continued)

PLAYER	TD	PAT	FG	TOTAL	YEAR(S) SCORED
Herd, Chuck	3	0	0	18	1971-72-73
Hess, Harold	1	0	0	6	1919
Hewitt, Earl	1	0	0	4	1901
Higgins, Bob	1	0	0	6	1919
Hoak, Dick	(see Series Touchdown Passes)				
Hoffman, Bob	(see Series Touchdown Passes)				
Hoggard, Dennie	1	0	0	6	1947
Horst, Tim	1	0	0	6	1968
Huber, Bill	0	1	0	2	1964
Hufnagel, John	-	-	-	-	-
Hull, John	0	5	0	5	1970
Hull, Tom	1	0	0	6	1973
Irwin, Mike	1	1	0	7	1966
Jacks, Al	(see Series Touchdown Passes)				
Jackson, Kenny	3	0	0	18	1980-81
Joachim, Steve	(see Series Touchdown Passes)				
Joe, Larry	1	0	0	6	1942
Jonas, Don	1	4	0	10	1958
Kane, Billy	1	0	0	6	1956
Kerr, Jimmy	1	0	0	6	1960
Klingensmith, Gary	1	0	0	6	1963
Kochman, Roger	2	2	0	14	1961-62
Kunit, Don	2	0	0	12	1965
Kwalick, Ted	2	0	0	12	1966-68
Lamb, Levi	0	0	1	3	1914
Lasich, George	1	0	0	6	1930
Leonard, Bill	1	4	1	13	1950-51-52
Liske, Pete	(see Series Touchdown Passes)				
Lucyk, Dan	1	0	0	6	1967
Markiewicz, Ron	1	0	0	6	1957
Martin, Percival	0	2	0	4	1900
Mauthe, Pete	2	5	2	23	1911-12
McCleary, Bull	2	1	0	11	1906-09
McCown, Dick	1	0	0	6	1943
McGee, George	1	0	0	5	1904
McIlveen, Irish	5	0	0	25	1902-03-05
McMillan, Bill	1	0	0	6	1931
McNaughton, Dave	2	0	0	12	1964-65
Meade, Mike	1	0	0	6	1981
Menhardt, Herb	0	2	1	5	1979-80
Metro, Joe	0	1	0	1	1936
Miller, Shorty	1	0	0	6	1912
Mitchell, Lydell	3	0	0	18	1971
Mitinger, Bob	1	0	0	6	1960
Moore, Lenny	1	0	0	6	1953
Nagle, Bob	2	0	0	12	1972-73

INDIVIDUAL SCORING (Continued)

PLAYER	TD	PAT	FG	TOTAL	YEAR(S) SCORED
**Neal	0	0	0	2	1893
Neff, Norm	2	0	0	12	1958
North, Paul	1	0	0	6	1958
Nye, Dirk	1	0	0	6	1964
O'Bara, Vince	0	3	0	3	1950
Pae, Dick	1	0	0	6	1959
Parsons, Bob	1	0	0	6	1971
Patrick, John	1	0	1	9	1939-40
Petchell, Elwood	1	0	0	6	1947
Petrella, Pepper	3	0	0	18	1941
Pittman, Charlie	6	0	0	36	1967-68-69
Plum, Milt	0	1	0	1	1956
Pollock, Ban	0	2	0	2	1937-39
Powell, Junior	1	0	0	6	1961
Prevost, Jules	0	0	1	3	1924
Rados, Tony	1	0	0	6	1953
Ramich, Joel	1	0	0	6	1970
Reitz, Mike	0	3	0	3	1969
Rickenbach, Bob	1	0	0	6	1972
Robinson, Mark	1	0	0	6	1981
Roepke, Johnny	1	1	0	7	1925-26
Rollins, Steve	(see Series Touchdown Passes)				
Rowell, Buddy	2	0	0	12	1952-53
Russell, Sam	0	2	0	2	1901
Sandusky, Jerry	1	0	0	6	1963
Scholl, Henry	4	0	0	16	1900-01
Schuster, Dick	0	0	2	6	1923
Scott, Jim	1	0	0	6	1972
Seeley, Brit	1	0	0	5	1902
Sherman, Tom	0	4	0	4	1965-66
Sherry, Jack	1	0	0	6	1954
Shuman, Tom	(see Series Touchdown Passes)				
Smaltz, Bill	1	1	1	10	1939-41
Smith, Andy	1	2	0	7	1902
Smith, Mike	1	0	0	6	1968
Stahley, Skip	1	0	0	6	1929
Stellatella, Sam	0	1	0	1	1959
Stuart, W. A.	1	0	0	4	1893
Suhey, Matt	1	0	0	6	1979
Szajna, Bob	(see Series Touchdown Passes)				
Thompson, Irv	3	0	0	15	1903
Torrey, Bob	1	0	0	6	1976
Torris, Buddy	1	0	0	6	1961
Urbanik, Tom	2	0	0	12	1964
Unger, Frank	1	0	0	6	1918
Van Lenton, Wilbur	0	2	0	2	1942

INDIVIDUAL SCORING (Continued)

PLAYER	TD	PAT	FG	TOTAL	YEAR(S) SCORED
Ventresco, Ralph	1	0	0	6	1941
Very, Dexter	1	0	0	6	1912
Vitiello, Alberto	0	14	0	14	1971-72
Vorhis, Larry	0	0	3	12	1908
Vukmar, Bob	1	0	0	6	1966
Warner, Curt	1	0	0	6	1979
Way, Charley	1	0	0	6	1919
Weitzel, Bob	1	0	0	6	1946
Weston, Ken	0	1	0	1	1925
White, Jack	1	0	0	6	1965
Whitworth, Ed	3	0	0	12	1901
Williams, Bobby	2	0	0	12	1947
Williams, Tom	1	0	0	6	1974
Yeckley, George	0	1	0	1	1905

*played with both Penn State and Pitt during WW II
**2-point safety

Note: scoring includes 4, 5 and 6-point touchdowns; one and 2-pt. conversions;
four and 3-pt. field goals.

PITT INDIVIDUAL SCORING**
1893-1981

PLAYER	TD	PAT	FG	TOTAL	YEAR(S) SCORED*
Abraham, Bill	1	0	0	6	1946
Anderson, John	1	0	0	6	1922
Bagamery, Ambrose	0	3	0	3	1955-56
Baker, Ed	1	1	0	7	1930
Bestwick, Bob	(see Series Touchdown Passes)				
Blanda, Paul	0	1	0	1	1951
Block, Leslie	1	0	0	6	1971
Bohren, Karl	1	0	0	6	1923
Bolkovac, Nick	1	4	0	10	1948-49-50
Bonelli, Ernest	0	2	0	2	1940
Booth, Bullet	2	4	0	16	1927
Brown, Jesse	1	0	0	6	1924
Campbell, J. F.	2	0	0	11	1907-08
Campbell, Jim	1	0	0	6	1950
Cassiano, Dick	3	0	0	18	1938

PLAYER	TD	PAT	FG	TOTAL	YEAR(S) SCORED
Cavanaugh, Matt	1	0	0	6	1977
Cecconi, Bimbo	2	0	0	12	1949
Chess, Paul.	1	0	0	6	1951
Chester, Dewey.	1	0	0	6	1965
Clark, Fred	0	1	1	4	1965
Clark, Jim	1	0	0	6	1931
Clemens, Bob.	1	0	0	6	1959
Collins, ...	1	0	0	6	1914
Collins, Dwight.	2	0	0	12	1981
Coury, Bill	0	2	0	2	1946
Cox, Fred	1	4	1	13	1959-60-61
Cutri, Rocco	0	5	0	5	1931
Daddio, Bill.	0	5	0	5	1936-38
Davies, Tom	1	4	0	10	1918
DePasqua, Carl.	(see Series Touchdown Passes)				
DeRosa, Nick	1	0	0	6	1950
Dorsett, Tony.	4	0	0	24	1973-74-76
Edgar, Joe.	0	2	0	2	1904
Edwards, Charles	0	1	0	1	1928
Englert, Bill.	2	1	0	14	1972
Esposito, Tony	3	0	0	18	1968-69-70
Everett, Snuffy	0	2	0	2	1981
Ferris, Dennis	1	0	0	6	1970
Flanagan, Hoot.	2	0	0	12	1922-23
Flanigan, James.	1	0	0	6	1966
Galvin, Ralph	0	1	0	1	1910
Gaugler, Gene.	1	0	0	6	1944
Gaustad, Steve.	1	0	0	6	1978
Goldberg, Marshall.	3	0	0	18	1937
Gougler, R. A.	2	3	1	18	1915-17
Grier, Bobby	1	0	0	6	1955
Gustafson, Andrew	2	2	1	17	1924-25
Gustine, Frankie.	(see Series Touchdown Passes)				
Gwosden, Milo	2	2	0	14	1923-24
Hagan, Jimmy	1	0	0	6	1927
Hasson, ...	1	0	0	6	1931
Hastings, Sandy.	3	3	5	36	1914-15-16
Havern, Dave	(see Series Touchdown Passes)				
Heller, Warren	2	0	0	12	1930
Hogan, John.	(see Series Touchdown Passes)				
Hood, Franklin	1	0	0	6	1928
Hoblitzell, R. D..	0	1	0	1	1907
James, Ed.	(see Series Touchdown Passes)				
Jastrzembski, Steve	1	0	0	6	1961
Jenkins, John	1	0	0	6	1961
Jones, Edgar.	1	1	0	7	1941
Jones, Gordon	1	0	0	6	1977

PLAYER	TD	PAT	FG	TOTAL	YEAR(S) SCORED
Jones, Joe	1	0	0	6	1966
Kaliden, Bill	(see Series Touchdown Passes)				
Kinsley, Eric	0	1	0	1	1972
Kracum, George	2	0	0	12	1940
Leeson, Rick	3	1	1	22	1961-63
Long, Carson	0	4	4	16	1973-74-76
Longo, Bob	2	1	0	14	1965-66
Lucas, Ken	(see Series Touchdown Passes)				
Lungren, Cy	(see Series Touchdown Passes)				
Marino, Dan	(see Series Touchdown Passes)				
Marshall,	1	0	0	4	1896
Matesic, Dick	2	0	0	12	1931
Martha, Paul	1	0	0	6	1963
Mazurek, Fred	1	0	0	6	1963
McCain, Joe	0	0	1	3	1968
McCarter, H. C.	1	0	0	6	1917
McCutcheon, D.	1	0	0	6	1924
McKnight, Barry	2	0	0	12	1965
McLaren, George	4	0	0	24	1917-18
McMillan, Randy	3	0	0	18	1979
Medich, George	1	0	0	6	1967
Mehl, O. H.	2	0	0	10	1904
Merkovsky, Elmer	0	1	0	1	1937
Moyer, Steve	2	0	0	12	1971
Neft, Peter	1	0	0	6	1955
Ostrowski, Stan	1	0	0	6	1972
Parkinson, Tom	4	2	0	26	1928-29
Patrick, Frank	3	1	1	22	1935-36-37
Pryor, Benjie	1	0	0	6	1980
Reinhold, Chuck	1	0	0	6	1958
Richards, Dave	1	0	0	5	1910
Riddle, Fred	1	0	0	6	1957
Rife, Gerald	1	0	0	6	1966
Robinson, Jimmy Joe	2	0	0	12	1945-49
Rooney, James	0	4	1	7	1926-28
Rosborough, Michael	1	0	0	6	1956
Roussos, Mike	0	3	0	3	1944-45
Salata, A. J.	1	0	0	6	1925
Salvaterra, Corny	1	0	0	6	1955
Scherer, Dick	1	0	0	6	1957
Schmidt, Joe	1	0	0	6	1926
Schmidt, Judd	2	0	0	10	1904
Schubert, Mark	0	4	4	16	1977-78-79
Scisly, Joe	1	0	0	6	1958
Seaman, Norton	0	4	0	4	1957-58
Sharockman, Ed	1	0	0	6	1958
Sies, Dale	0	1	0	1	1917
Simms,	2	0	0	12	1931
Skladany, Leo	1	0	0	6	1946

INDIVIDUAL SCORING (Continued)

PLAYER	TD	PAT	FG	TOTAL	YEAR(S) SCORED
Sniscak, Bernie	1	0	0	6	1944
Souchak, Frank	0	3	0	3	1936-37
Spicko, Joe	0	1	1	4	1969-70
Stebbins, Harold	2	0	0	12	1936
Toerper, Todd	1	0	0	6	1972
Toncic, Ivan	1	1	0	7	1957-59
Thurbon, Bob	2	0	0	12	1938-40
Traficant, Jim	(see Series Touchdown Passes)				
Trocano, Rick	1	0	0	6	1980
Trout, Dave	0	2	0	2	1980
Uansa, Toby	2	0	0	12	1928
Urban, John	1	0	0	6	1936
Wagner, Hube	1	0	0	5	1910
Walker, Elliott	2	0	0	12	1975-76
Warriner, Chris	2	0	0	12	1950-51
Welch, Gibby	4	0	0	24	1925-26-27
West, Walt	1	0	0	6	1942
Williams, Harold	0	2	0	2	1922
Williamson, G. M.	1	1	0	7	1913
Wood, Johnny	1	0	0	6	1936

Note: scoring includes 4, 5 and 6-point touchdowns; one and 2-pt. conversions; four and 3-pt. field goals.   **Pitt has 22 miscellaneous points scored; players unidentified.

LONG SCORING PLAYS

(50 yards or greater)

RANK	YARDS	PLAYER-TEAM	TYPE OF PLAY	YEAR
1	100	Toby Uansa, Pitt	Kickoff return	1928
2	95	Curt Warner, PSU	Kickoff return	1979
3	93	Bernie Sniscak, Pitt	Kickoff return	1944
4	91	Mark Robinson, PSU	Interception	1981
5	90	Larry Joe, PSU	Kickoff return	1942
5	90	Jimmy Joe Robinson, Pitt	Punt return	1945
7	86	Fred Cox, Pitt	Run from scrimmage	1959
8	80	Gibby Welch, Pitt	Run from scrimmage	1925
8	80	Warren Heller, Pitt	Run from scrimmage	1930
10	79	Lenny Moore, PSU	Run from scrimmage	1953
11	75	Sandy Hastings, Pitt	Run via lateral	1916
11	75	Bob Higgins, PSU	Pass from Harold Hess	1919
13	70	Karl Bohren, Pitt	Run from scrimmage	1923
14	67	Judd Schmidt, Pitt	Run from scrimmage	1904
14	67	G. M. Williamson, Pitt	Run from scrimmage	1913
16	65	Matt Suhey, PSU	Run from scrimmage	1979
17	63	Ted Kwalick, PSU	Pass from Chuck Burkhart	1968
18	62	Corny Salvaterra, Pitt	Run from scrimmage	1955
19	60	Dick Matesic, Pitt	Interception	1931
19	60	Bill Leonard, PSU	Interception	1950
21	59	Gary Hayman, PSU	Punt return	1972
21	59	Randy McMillan, Pitt	Pass from Dan Marino	1979
23	58	Jimmy Joe Robinson, Pitt	Pass from Bimbo Cecconi	1949
24	56	Carl Forkham, PSU	Run from scrimmage	1903
24	56	Roger Kochman, PSU	Pass from Pete Liske	1962
26	54	Gibby Welch, Pitt	Run from scrimmage	1926
27	52	Irish McIlveen, PSU	Run from scrimmage	1903
27	52	Bob Parsons, PSU	Pass from John Hufnagel	1971
27	52	Mike Guman, PSU	Punt return	1977
30	51	Pete Mauthe, PSU	Field goal	1912
31	50	Hube Wagner, Pitt	Punt return	1910
31	50	Carson Long, Pitt	Field goal	1973
31	50	Chris Bahr, PSU	Field goal	1974

SERIES TOUCHDOWN PASSES

NO.	PASSER-RECEIVER	TEAM	YARDS	YEAR
1.	Dexter Very-Pete Mauthe	PSU	32	1912
* 2.	Larry Conover-Charlie Way	PSU	20	1917
3.	Harold Hess-Bob Higgins	PSU	75	1919
4.	Hoot Flanagan-John Anderson	Pitt	15	1922
5.	Karl Bohren-Hoot Flanagan	Pitt	15	1923
6.	Cy Lungren-Johnny Roepke	PSU	34	1925
7.	Franklin Hood-Ed Baker	Pitt	2	1930
8.	Marshall Goldberg-Harold Stebbins	Pitt	25	1936
9.	Steve Rollins-Spike Alter	PSU	30	1937
10.	Edgar Jones-Bob Thurbon	Pitt	20	1940
11.	Carl DePasqua-Leo Skladany	Pitt	7	1946
12.	Bimbo Cecconi-Jimmy Joe Robinson	Pitt	58	1949
13.	Bob Bestwick-Chris Warriner	Pitt	14	1950
14.	Bob Bestwick-Nick DeRosa	Pitt	25	1950
15.	Bob Szajna-Jesse Arnelle	PSU	9	1951
16.	Bob Bestwick-Chris Warriner	Pitt	32	1951
17.	Bob Hoffman-Jack Sherry	PSU	19	1954
18.	Corny Salveterra-Michael Rosborough	Pitt	18	1956
19.	Bill Kaliden-Dick Scherer	Pitt	45	1957
20.	Al Jacks-Paul North	PSU	9	1957
21.	Eddie Caye-Ron Markiewicz	PSU	1	1957
22.	Al Jacks-Norm Neff	PSU	9	1958
23.	Dick Hoak-Norm Neff	PSU	8	1958
24.	Butch Hall-Jim Kerr	PSU	30	1960
25.	Dick Hoak-Bob Mitinger	PSU	3	1960
26.	Paul Martha-John Jenkins	Pitt	8	1961
27.	Butch Hall-Al Gursky	PSU	23	1961
28.	Butch Hall-Junior Powell	PSU	48	1961
29.	Jim Traficant-Steve Jastrzembski	Pitt	6	1961
30.	Pete Liske-Roger Kochman	PSU	56	1962
31.	Pete Liske-Al Gursky	PSU	18	1962
32.	Pete Liske-Jerry Sandusky	PSU	9	1963
33.	Pete Liske-Don Caum	PSU	10	1963
34.	Ken Lucas-Bob Longo	Pitt	41	1965
35.	Tom Sherman-Jack Curry	PSU	30	1966
36.	Tom Sherman-Ted Kwalick	PSU	3	1966
37.	Ed James-Joe Jones	Pitt	5	1966
38.	Tom Sherman-Bobby Campbell	PSU	9	1966
39.	Jack White-Bob Vukmar	PSU	11	1966
40.	Ed James-Bob Longo	Pitt	6	1966
41.	Ed James-Gerold Rife	Pitt	32	1966
42.	Tom Sherman-Don Abbey	PSU	23	1967
43.	Tom Sherman-Don Abbey	PSU	5	1967
44.	Tom Sherman-Jack Curry	PSU	16	1967
45.	Tom Sherman-Dan Lucyk	PSU	5	1967
46.	Frankie Gustine-George Medich	Pitt	3	1967
47.	Chuck Burkhart-Ted Kwalick	PSU	63	1968

SERIES TOUCHDOWN PASSES (Continued)

NO.	PASSER-RECEIVER	TEAM	YARDS	YEAR
48.	Mike Cooper-Tim Horst	PSU	19	1968
49.	John Hufnagel-Bob Parsons	PSU	52	1971
50.	John Hufnagel-Chuck Herd	PSU	49	1971
51.	Dave Havern-Steve Moyer	Pitt	27	1971
52.	Dave Havern-Steve Moyer	Pitt	37	1971
53.	Steve Joachim-Gary Debes	PSU	13	1971
54.	Dave Havern-Leslie Block	Pitt	3	1971
55.	John Hufnagel-Jim Scott	PSU	31	1972
56.	John Hufnagel-Dave Bland	PSU	21	1972
57.	John Hufnagel-Chuck Herd	PSU	41	1972
58.	Tom Shuman-Bob Rickenbach	PSU	13	1972
59.	John Hogan-Bill Englert	Pitt	12	1972
60.	John Hogan-Todd Toerper	Pitt	33	1972
61.	John Hogan-Stan Ostrowski	Pitt	13	1972
62.	John Hogan-Bill Englert	Pitt	1	1972
63.	Tom Shuman-Chuck Herd	PSU	23	1973
64.	Tom Shuman-Jim Eaise	PSU	23	1974
65.	Tom Shuman-Jim Eaise	PSU	35	1974
66.	Chuck Fusina-Bob Torrey	PSU	21	1976
67.	Matt Cavanaugh-Gordon Jones	Pitt	17	1977
68.	Rick Trocano-Steve Gaustad	Pitt	16	1978
69.	Dan Marino-Randy McMillan	Pitt	59	1979
70.	Rick Trocano-Benjie Pryor	Pitt	16	1980
71.	Todd Blackledge-Kenny Jackson	PSU	13	1980
72.	Dan Marino-Dwight Collins	Pitt	28	1981
73.	Dan Marino-Dwight Collins	Pitt	9	1981
74.	Todd Blackledge-Kenny Jackson	PSU	42	1981
75.	Todd Blackledge-Kenny Jackson	PSU	45	1981

*Triple Pass

PITT vs. PENN STATE

AT

	G	W	L	T
Exposition Park (Pittsburgh)	6	2	4	0
Forbes Field (Pittsburgh)	17	10	5	2
Pitt Stadium (Pittsburgh)	38	21	16	1
Three Rivers Stadium	3	1	2	0
TOTALS IN PITTSBURGH	64	34	27	3
Beaver Field (State College)	9	2	7	0
Beaver Stadium (State College)	8	2	6	0
TOTALS IN STATE COLLEGE	17	4	13	0

PITT COACHES vs. PENN STATE

COACH	PERIOD	G	W	L	T
1. Anson Harrold	1893	1	0	1	0
2. George Hoskins	1896	1	0	1	0
3. Dr. Roy Jackson	1900	1	0	1	0
4. Wilbur Hockensmith	1901	1	0	1	0
5. Fred Crolius	1902	1	0	1	0
6. Arthur Mosse	1903-05	3	1	2	0
7. E. R. Wingard	1906	1	0	1	0
8. John Moorhead	1907	1	1	0	0
9. Joe Thompson	1908-12	5	1	4	0
10. Joe Duff	1913-14	2	2	0	0
11. Pop Warner	1915-23	9	6	1	2
12. Jock Sutherland	1924-38	12	12	0	
13. Charles Bowser	1939-42	4	1	3	0
14. Clark Shaughnessy	1943-45	3	2	1	0
15. Wesley Fesler	1946	1	1	0	
16. Walt Milligan	1947-49	3	2	1	0
17. Len Casanova	1950	1	0	1	0
18. Tom Hamilton	1951	1	1	0	0
19. Lowell Dawson	1952-53	2	0	2	0
20. Dawson & Hamilton	1954	1	0	1	0
21. John Michelosen	1955-65	11	5	5	1
22. Dave Hart	1966-68	3	0	3	0
23. Carl DePasqua	1969-72	4	0	4	0
24. Johnny Majors	1973-76	4	1	3	0
25. Jackie Sherrill	1977-81	5	2	3	0

PENN STATE COACHES vs. PITT

COACH	PERIOD	G	W	L	T
1. George Hoskins	1893	1	1	0	0
2. Dr. Sam Newton	1896	1	1	0	0
3. Pop Golden	1900-02	3	3	0	0
4. Dan Reed	1903	1	1	0	0
5. Tom Fennell	1904-06	3	2	1	0
6. Bill Hollenback	1909, 1911-14	5	2	3	0
7. Jack Hollenback	1910	1	0	1	0
8. Dick Harlow	1915-17	3	0	3	0
9. Hugo Bezdek	1918-29	12	1	9	2
10. Bob Higgins	1930-48	16	5	11	0
11. Joe Bedenk	1949	1	0	1	0
12. Rip Engle	1950-65	16	9	6	1
13. Joe Paterno	1966-82	16	13	3	0

SERIES RECORDS

RUSHING, longest play	Jimmy Robinson, Pitt 90 (1945)
100-YARD game	Tony Dorsett, Pitt 224 (1976)
PASSING, longest play	Bob Higgins, Penn State 75 (1919)
PASSING, total yards	Dave Havern, Pitt 314 (1968)
PASSING, TDs one game	Tom Sherman, Penn State 4 (1967), John Hogan, Pitt 4 (1972)
PASSING, thrown	Dave Havern, Pitt 51 (1968)
PASSING, completions	Dave Havern, Pitt 29 (1968)
PASSING, interceptions	Bimbo Cecconi, Pitt 3 (1949), Henry Ford, Pitt 3 (1953)
PASSING, total yards	Penn State, 329 (1972)
RECEIVING, total yards	Kenny Jackson, Penn State 158 (1981)
RECEIVING, one player	Harry Orszulak, Pitt 16 (1968)
TOTAL OFFENSE, yards	Butch Hall, Penn State 266 (256 pass) (1961)
TOTAL OFFENSE, team	Penn State, 546 (1966)
KICKOFF, long return	Toby Uansa, Pitt 100 (1928)
PUNTS, long return	Dennis Onkotz, Penn State 71 (1969)
PUNTS, long	Wayne Corbett, Penn State 67 (1965)
FIELD GOALS, one game	Chris Bahr, Penn State 4 (1974)
FIELD GOALS, 50-yards	Pete Mauthe, Penn State 51 (1912)
INTERCEPTIONS, long return	Mark Robinson, Penn State 91 (1981)
POINTS, one game, one player	Carl Forkum, Penn State 38 (1903)
POINTS, one team, shutout	Penn State, 59 (1903)
POINTS, one team	Penn State, 65 (1968)
POINTS, both teams	76 (PSU 49-27) (1972)

COACHING RIVALRIES

Pop Warner vs. Harlow, Bezdek

PERIOD	G	W	L	T
1915-23	9	6	1	2

Jock Sutherland vs. Bezdek, Higgins

PERIOD	G	W	L	T
1924-38	12	12	0	0

Rip Engle vs. John Michelosen

PERIOD	G	W	L	T
1955-65	11	5	5	1

Joe Paterno vs. Johnny Majors

PERIOD	G	W	L	T
1973-76	4	3	1	0

Joe Paterno vs. Jackie Sherrill

PERIOD	G	W	L	T
1977-81	5	3	2	0

The Author

Tim Panaccio has covered college and professional sports for six years. He was a sportswriter with the *Philadelphia Journal* until the paper's closure in 1981. Prior to 1979, Panaccio worked at the *Pittsburgh Post-Gazette* and began his career in 1976 with the *Philadelphia Inquirer*. He is also the author of a short book, "The Comeback Kids," a story of the 1980 World Champion Phillies. Panaccio is married to the former Carla Tolina. Along with their son Nicolas, the Panaccio's live in Philadelphia.